LILLIAN COHEN KOVAR,
author of this book,
is Research Sociologist,
The William Alanson White Institute,
New York.
She is also the author of
Statistical Methods for Social Scientists.

FACES OF THE ADOLESCENT GIRL

FACES OF THE ADOLESCENT GIRL

Lillian Cohen Kovar

The William Alanson White Institute

A SPECTRUM BOOK

PRENTICE-HALL, INC.
Englewood Cliffs, N. J.

Library of Congress Catalog Card Number: 68-17821

PRINTED IN THE UNITED STATES OF AMERICA

Current printing (last digit)
10   9   8   7   6   5   4   3   2   1

To ROBBY and LEO
My First Mentor and My Last

PREFACE

My interest in studying the adolescent girl developed initially out of an attempt to evaluate what was happening to girls who were committed to various juvenile delinquency institutions throughout New York State. As a staff member of the Juvenile Delinquency Evaluation Project for the City of New York, I visited institutions to which girls were committed, observed their activities, and spoke with the staff and with the girls. After spending several months at each institution, I did not feel that I had caught the girls' experience of institutionalization.

To get closer to the experiences of institutionalized girls, I became a participant observer on the adolescent girls' wards of three mental hospitals. In addition, in the process of formulating a typology of adolescent girls, it became necessary to interview girls in the community.

The participant observation in the hospital and the interviewing in the community extended over a period of years. Since the completion of the study in 1965, the adolescent scene has, in some measure, changed, at least on important peripheries. Despite this, I think that for purposes of analysis the framework of conformity-deviance-autonomy developed in this study remains valid.

Many persons helped to make this study possible. The research was supported by grant M-2452 from the National Institute of Mental Health and by a psychiatric fellowship from the New York

State Department of Mental Hygiene. I am especially indebted to Dr. Lauretta Bender, Principal Research Psychiatrist in Child Psychiatry and Departmental Consultant, New York State Department of Mental Hygiene, whose efforts in my behalf enabled me to gain entrée and to pursue my studies in the state hospitals. I am grateful to the many staff members at the three hospitals and at the community centers who gave of their time and knowledge. To the girls in the hospitals and in the community who usually accepted their roles as guinea pigs with good humor, my thanks and appreciation. Finally, my husband, Leo, was for me the best of all possible critics, combining a powerful intellectual vision with an acute sensitivity to detail. His insights permeate the book.

Lillian Cohen Kovar
The William Alanson White Institute
New York City

CONTENTS

FACES OF THE
ADOLESCENT
GIRL

one

INTRODUCTION

The adolescent girl shows many faces. Five of them
are described briefly below.

Elizabeth indicates that "in her whole being a girl would want
to follow the judgment of her mother." Her thinking on most matters regarding school, dating, sex relations, or religion follows closely
what her mother says is good and right.

In contrast, Ann feels that her mother has never had time for
her, and her ideas and values are defined and circumscribed by her
peers. She disparages such seeming nonconformists as the anarchic
bohemians with their "odd" dress, their poetry readings, and their
"lack of morals."

Ruth, audacious and intellectually astute, flouts the rules that
her family and her dominant peers espouse. She fails in school, she
dresses in off-beat fashion, she runs away with one man and then
another, and finally she lands in the mental hospital.

Fay, too, runs away and she becomes sexually promiscuous, initially to provoke her parents and also to experience the thrill of
momentary acceptance by another person.

Suzanne participates actively in civil-rights activities, dates regularly, and begins to prepare for college and a career as an illustrator of children's books. In whatever she does, she displays a spontaneity and a freedom to act out of her own choice.

The last of these girls I call autonomous and it is my thesis that only the autonomous girl is mentally healthy. Already in high school she is a strong individualist who seems potentially capable of forming intimate and loving relationships.

My initial experience in looking at girls from the point of view of autonomy or its absence consisted of the observation of girls in mental hospitals. I spent three to four months as a participant observer in each of three mental hospitals located in the metropolitan area of New York City—one private and two state hospitals. I played and talked with the girls, ate with them, and slept on the ward with two of the groups at least one night a week. The girls at the hospitals provided the major source of insight and became the "experimental" group in the design of the study.

If we look at girls as autonomous or else as conformist or deviant, the hospital girls were all deviant. Their behavior deviated from the norms of their families or communities in such fashion that hospitalization was regarded as necessary. Without some form of "control" group, observations of the hospital girls alone were insufficient to delineate the nature of autonomy in adolescence. Therefore, in order to include conformists and autonomous girls in the study, adolescents outside the hospital were added to the original sample. They paralleled the hospital girls in class and race but included a larger proportion of middle-class white Protestant girls. Girls striving for autonomy were specifically sought out. The girls from outside the hospital are referred to as the community sample.

In all, I studied 151 girls, 72 in the community through intensive interviews and 79 in the three mental hospitals through participant observation. I took no notes in the presence of the hospital girls but maintained a running record of everything I observed and remembered that was related to my areas of interest. Standard interview techniques were used in the community sample. A description of the samples is given in Chapter Two.

The concept of autonomy became the core around which a typology of adolescent girls evolved. The girl who lacked autonomy was either deviant, often in the ways encountered at the hospital, or else she conformed excessively, in ways that I was to observe among girls in the community.

It became evident as my observations continued that the concept of autonomy required a complementary concept to refer to the girl's relations with others, for the nature and extent of a girl's autonomy was dependent on, and was a complement of, her relations with others, both past and present. Thus "relation" was added to "autonomy" in the conceptual framework for observation and analysis. These concepts are described below.[1]

AUTONOMY AND RELATION

The *autonomous process* I define as a temporary withdrawal from relations with others, a withdrawal (always psychological but not necessarily physical) that helps to reinforce one as a separate and distinct personality in personal relations. To illustrate, the girl who is autonomous expresses her own feelings (her mother cannot tell her how to feel), she thinks her own thoughts (and not necessarily those her teacher and textbook impose upon her), she observes, she reads, she learns, she dreams, she lets herself go in solitude and repose and brings these feelings and this knowledge to her relations with others. The autonomous process is at all times either potentially or actually in the service of positive relationships. (And so the social isolate or the dictator, however strong an individualist, cannot be regarded as autonomous.)

The complement to autonomy is *relation*. Relations with others that are positive can be looked upon as being either "reciprocal" or "personal." A girl learns to reciprocate, giving "this for that," and such reciprocity is a necessary basis for all personal relations. But in addition she hopefully will soon experience relations that are more intimate and loving. She will see others in their personal qualities and capacities, and not as she would like them to be nor according to how they perform or what they provide. She will respond passionately to others. She will trust and have faith in them and they in her, so that each dares to step beyond the reciprocal

[1] Angyal speaks about autonomy and homonomy as man's two basic strivings. For his development of these concepts, *see* Andras Angyal, *Neurosis and Treatment: A Holistic Theory*, E. Hanfmann and R.M. Jones (eds.) (New York: John Wiley & Sons, Inc., 1965).

role relationship and act out of personal choice, assured of being continued in the relationship.[2]

Much more has been written about the adolescent girl's relations with others than about her autonomy. Her relations with her peers —first with other girls and then with boys—have been stressed in the literature on adolescence. It is during adolescence that a girl's bond to her biological family weakens considerably and she begins to look for a mate and to prepare herself for marriage and a new family.

However, a girl's positive relations with others are usually "reciprocal" and not "personal." With other girls her relationships are somewhat ambivalent, and rarely does she achieve intimacy and love in her relationships with boys during her high school years. She may date boys regularly and may neck and pet with them or go further in her sexual relations but these are not relations of intimacy and love.

There is good reason for her lack of intimate personal relationships. Such relationships can occur only between two (or more) autonomous persons, each preserving his separateness and individuality. The adolescent girl is not yet an autonomous person.

It is my premise that the extension of autonomy is crucial during adolescence if a girl is to prepare herself for the love and intimacy of adulthood. To undertake autonomous pursuits, she cannot enter adolescence crippled by a heritage of troubled relations within her family from her earliest years. I shall give here a brief capitulation of what the girl should have experienced in her family if she is to be "ready" to take advantage of adolescence.

The genesis of autonomy

From a very few months of age, the young child seems to find pleasure in doing things for herself. "By me," "by myself,"

[2] *See* John MacMurray, *The Self as Agent* (London: Faber & Faber, Ltd., 1957), and *Persons in Relation* (London: Faber & Faber, Ltd., 1961). These are Volumes I and II of MacMurray's Gifford Lectures, 1953-1954, given under the title "The Form of the Personal." *See also* Martin Buber, *Between Man and Man,* trans. Ronald Gregor Smith (London: Kegan Paul, 1947), pp. 184 ff.; and Maurice S. Friedman, *Martin Buber: The Life of Dialogue* (New York: Harper & Row, Publishers, 1960; first published by the University of Chicago Press, 1955).

she soon indicates. Her acquiring of skills has the character of play. She learns skills for their own sake, for the pleasure in doing. She learns to crawl, then to walk, and in other ways learns to gain pleasure from her body—for example, to suck and to bite, to expel her feces. She learns to distinguish and to make sounds, to discriminate between shapes and between colors, to relate sight and touch, then on to wider, more comprehensive skills through childhood and adolescence when she learns, for example, how to fill out application forms, how to write a book report, how to approach a boy and talk with him.

The skills are learned from and in relation to other people, first to the mothering one, then to the teacher and to peers. The girl returns continually to receive confirmation of her productions, and essentially, of herself. It is her experience of the confrontation with and the confirmation from others of her own personal product that helps to establish the distinction between herself and others. She can say, "This is mine, which I myself produced, apart from all others." She develops a sense of power and self-direction.

She learns that limits are set to acts of self-assertion that are injurious to others. The person who sets the limits is initially her parent who loves her. Gradually she comes to identify with the victims of her own aggression and to set limits to her own autonomy.

During adolescence she dates boys and at the same time she gains knowledge of and feeling for the world around her. She paints, joins a political club, becomes a cheerleader, reads extensively. Hopefully some of her interests and involvements will eventually coalesce with those of a mate. If she wants to find a husband with whom she can have a personal relationship, she must train herself to be autonomous as well as loving. In developing her individuality and her ability to give and receive love, she is also preparing herself to be a mother, capable of withdrawing from and returning to the relationship with her own children and thus nurturing in them the potentiality for independence as well as personal relation.

That autonomy is a necessary precondition for the intimacy of adulthood has been widely postulated by others. In Angyal's words, ". . . bringing one's best to a loving relationship requires not only a capacity for self-surrender but also a degree of proficient mastery of one's world, of resourcefulness and self-reliance. Without these qualities one does not have much to offer the other, and the relationship may deteriorate into dependency and exploitation." [3]

Also Erik Erikson: ". . . the condition of a true twoness is that one must first become oneself." [4] "True 'engagement' with others is the result and the test of firm self-delineation." [5]

Helene Deutsch corroborates: ". . . the more completely a woman preserves her own personality, the more easily does she adjust herself to a man." [6]

Erich Fromm speaks of love ". . . as the union of the individual with others on the basis of the preservation of the individual self." [7]

And Robert MacIver affirms, "You must give yourself in love but you must not give yourself away." [8]

But autonomy is always only one side of the person. To achieve intimacy and love as an adult requires not only long experiences in autonomous pursuits but also long experiences in relationships of love.

The genesis of personal relations

The beginnings of loving relationships occur in infancy and early childhood when the daughter has, ideally, experienced unconditional love from her parents.

The baby's cry soon after birth might be considered the first call for help from others, the anticipated personal relation. The mothering one's response to the call, the baby's expression of delight in being cared for and receiving attention, and the consequent relationship of trust that is established between mother and child,

---

[3] Angyal, *op. cit.*, p. 29.

[4] Erik H. Erikson, "The Healthy Personality," in *Identity and the Life Cycle (Psychological Issues)*, Vol. I, No. 1 (New York: International Universities Press, 1959), p. 95.

[5] Erik H. Erikson, "The Problem of Ego Identity," in *Identity and the Life Cycle*, p. 124.

[6] Helene Deutsch, *The Psychology of Women* (New York: Grune & Stratton, Inc., 1944), Vol. I, p. 133.

[7] Erich Fromm, *Escape from Freedom* (New York: Holt, Rinehart & Winston, Inc., 1941), p. 261.

[8] Robert M. MacIver, *The Pursuit of Happiness* (New York: Simon and Schuster, Inc., 1955), p. 130.

is one prototype of what love is. The child has the experience of being the recipient of love from her parents who have given with no expectation of return (of one kind or another). She also experiences generosity. Her own spontaneous giving, to her little brother, perhaps, was responded to by her parents as important and not as trivial. From this early experience with receiving and giving love, she develops some sense of what she is looking for in her relations with others. If she has had no such experience, she cannot affirm herself as a person capable of loving and being loved.

She comes to learn that relationships, since they involve another, are always problematic, and never completely unconditional.[9] Not only does my mother, even, have incomplete knowledge of me, but she also has needs of her own and so she does not always consider my interests first.

A girl's relations with parents and siblings are soon interspersed with relations to peers. It is during preadolescence, at nine or ten, that for the first time a person other than herself, her chum, becomes of almost equal importance to her and she is now capable of seeing herself through her chum's eyes.[10] She is thus learning to give love, to "respond" to another, and she is learning to establish some detachment and look at herself as an object as she is seen by others.

During puberty, the girl turns more openly to boys and much of the thrill of adolescence comes from her infatuations.[11] With each successive infatuation she is, hopefully, beginning to perfect her personal relations. Achieving love is a slow process. She must establish a relationship with a boy that has the quality of the parent-child relationship, in its ideal form, and other essential ingredients. She must build up a body of shared experiences with another

[9] For an analysis of the problematic in human relationships, *see* MacMurray, *Persons in Relation.*

[10] *See* Harry Stack Sullivan, *The Interpersonal Theory of Psychiatry,* Helen Swick Perry and Mary Ladd Gawel (eds.) (New York: W. W. Norton & Company, Inc., 1953), pp. 245, 248.

[11] An infatuation is a mixture of the "lust dynamism" and the excitement of the social game in diverse combinations. Sullivan speaks about the "lust dynamism," the tensions pertaining to the genitals, as erupting in early adolescence (*op. cit.,* pp. 109, 263).

person who is starting at the same point and is engaged in the same search. She must learn that the rewards of fidelity to another human being are greater than the pleasures of momentary infatuation. She must become both a giver and a receiver at the same time. With recurrent withdrawals from relationships into autonomous pursuits and returns to relations, the girl gradually learns how to love.

Having introduced the concepts of autonomy and relation, I should like to apply these concepts to various types of adolescent girls.

A TYPOLOGY OF THE ADOLESCENT GIRL

The typology of the adolescent girl developed here is based on the extent and nature of a girl's autonomy and relations. These are empirical types that grew out of observation and interview. The girl labeled adult-oriented has too strong a relation with parents, with a consequent loss in autonomy; the peer-oriented girl, too strong a relation with peers. The delinquent searches compulsively for the relation she never had, and the anarchic bohemian, for the autonomy she feels she lacked. Only the autonomous girl has acquired in proper measure the beginnings of autonomy and personal relation.

I want to ask what "caused" girls to become these types. In trying to recreate from her early relations with family the probable genesis of a girl's type, I have used the concepts of "confirmation" and "affirmation." It is my thesis that a girl is *confirmed* by her family in a certain fashion and that she continues to *affirm* herself in the manner in which she was confirmed. A cycle is set up that is difficult to break without strong intervention or intercession. And so, at adolescence we see, for example, girls who have been confirmed as "good" (the adult-oriented type), girls confirmed as "bad" (the delinquent), girls confirmed as "peculiar" (the anarchic bohemian), and girls confirmed as "genuine" (the autonomous). Theoretically, the types of confirmation and consequent affirmation are limited only by the vision of the investigator.

My model is the autonomous girl. Her autonomy has been fostered by her parents and other significant persons from her earliest years. She was allowed from the beginning to set her own pace. Her initial spontaneous actions were responded to (i.e., "confirmed") by her parents as positive and genuine if they were not injurious to herself or others. Consequently, she begins from her earliest years to develop her individuality in her own unique way and to achieve some mastery and competence in areas of her choice. Though she is sensitive to the guidance of her family and later of her peers and teachers, within broad limits they do not intrude as the final authorities. She thinks and feels for herself. She is confirmed by her parents not only as a spontaneous individual but also as a person worthy of receiving unconditional love. Hence, she is not paralyzed into inaction by fear of failure or of rejection. Her action has a quality of daring and freedom. It emerges in partially unpredictable fashion, transcending what would be expected from her prescribed roles and differing in some significant way from that of her parents and peers.

She affirms herself as "genuine" to parents, to teachers, and to peers, and they continue to confirm her as a "genuine" person. She enters into relationships only with those others who continue her confirmation as "genuine." In adolescence, she is the *autonomous girl*. The autonomous ideal can be realized only when (1) family relations have promoted such an ideal; (2) social barriers (e.g., class, race) do not preclude confirmation as genuine by others outside the family;[12] and (3) others in her field of action are also functioning with autonomy.

With all other types of girls, something has gone wrong with the quantity and quality of relation and autonomy. There is the *adult-oriented girl* whose relationship with family has been overstressed and her autonomy curtailed. She is the girl who has not been allowed to engage in childish play and who very early puts aside childish ways and becomes the premature adult. She continually rechecks with her mother: Is this good? Is this right? Am I do-

[12] Ideally, a girl has accumulated experiences of the confirmation of her worth not only in her family but also in her community. She has been given the educational and social opportunities that should accrue to all by virtue of being "more simply human than otherwise." When her humanity is confirmed rather than her skin or her religion, she can affirm herself without shame or pretense. (The quote in this note is from Sullivan, *op. cit.*, p. 32.)

ing what you want? How shall I do this? The mother confirms only what she preconceives as good and right. The daughter is confirmed as the "good one" who obeys her mother and not as a child who plays and experiments and initiates in her own crude but important way. The daughter thus affirms herself as the "good one" who obeys the authority. She fears the new, the strange, and the unfamiliar. Life has meaning only under the umbrella of her parents, her teachers, and, later, her husband. She is always on the receiving end. She strives for what she thinks counts most to the world of adults. She may then well say, "I am the prudent one who studies or dates or plays but all in the manner that adults really think best."

This adult-oriented girl has received love conditioned on obedience. Though she affirms herself as the "good one," and not the "genuine one," she does have a cohesive relationship with her family. She is stereotyped by her peers as prudish and moralistic.[13]

Sometimes less emphasis is placed on the daughter's being good and obedient. In fact, the parent may show some indifference toward the girl's growth and direction and seem "absent" psychologically. She is confirmed by her parents as the "pretty one," a doll with curly hair or blue eyes or graceful bearing, or the "external one" who has a good voice or some other outward manifestation. She has been confirmed in an aspect of personhood but not as a person. The confirmation, whatever it is, has not been rooted in a strong personal relation between parent and child.

This girl was close to her siblings or peers from her earliest years. She turned excessively to her peers, with a consequent loss

[13] The adult-oriented girl's family would seem to resemble the family described by Bronfenbrenner, which, from the girl's earliest years, showered her with love and affection of a kind that made home a good place to go back to, if she remained a "good" girl (but not necessarily a good place to start out from, since it gave little impetus to autonomy). Parental discipline was probably love-oriented and aided the girl's development of strong internalized controls and consequent timidity, dependence, and conformity (more so probably than in her brother). Bronfenbrenner sees this family as primarily lower middle class. The adult-oriented girls described in my study come from a range of classes. *See* Urie Bronfenbrenner, "Some Familial Antecedents of Responsibility and Leadership in Adolescence," in L. Petrullo and B. M. Bass (eds.), *Leadership and Interpersonal Behavior* (New York: Holt, Rinehart & Winston, Inc., 1961), pp. 239-271.

of individual autonomy. The attention that was lacking at home she got from peers. She affirms herself with them as the "pretty one" or the "external one" and gains peer confirmation. I am my appearance, she may say, I am what I wear or how I act. She seeks out peers who will confirm her as she affirms herself, and she strives for what she thinks counts most to her peers—for example, appearance, fun. This is the characterization of the *peer-oriented girl.*[14]

A mother may show indifference to her daughter's growth and withdraw more frequently and more consistently than the mother of the peer-oriented girl. The daughter is "abandoned," if not physically, then at least psychologically. In a desperate effort to get the mother's attention, the daughter initiates "bad" behavior, at first possibly temper tantrums and later, louder and louder protests over her rejection through truanting and sexual deviance. The mother reacts by calling her "bad." After repeated initiations and confirmations of "bad" behavior, the girl's "bad" personification be-

[14] Recent sociological studies give two different versions of the adolescent girl—one, adult-oriented, and the other, peer-oriented.

The picture presented in a study of *Adolescent Girls* by the Survey Research Center, University of Michigan, based on a nationwide sample of girls, is the adult-oriented girl. Here, the girl generally has a stable relationship with her parents and readily accepts her mother as a model. By and large she considers her parents' guidance as necessary and legitimate. One-third of the nationwide sample say they want to be like their own mothers when they grow up, and more than half choose some woman within their family circles. Personal qualities such as kind, nice, and generous are most often mentioned as the reasons for the choice. The girl in this nationwide survey not only thinks it necessary for parents to make rules but also agrees with the specific rules they make. (*Adolescent Girls* [Ann Arbor: Survey Research Center, University of Michigan, 1957], pp. 7, 8, 9, 73, 80).

These findings are buttressed by a study of a well-to-do suburban community in Montreal, Canada, where few sharp conflicts were found between parents and their adolescent children. Family ties were close and the degree of basic family consensus high. *See* Frederick Elkin and William A. Westley, "The Myth of Adolescent Culture," *American Sociological Review*, Vol. XX (December 1955), pp. 682, 684.

Coleman, on the other hand, gives the picture of the peer-oriented girl. He points to the increased cultural distance between teen-age and adult culture in today's world. The language of the adolescent is becoming more and more different from that of the adult. (James S. Coleman, *The Adolescent Society* [New York: The Free Press, 1961], p. 3).

comes crystallized. Confirmed as "bad" by her parents, by herself, and later by her esteemed peers, she seeks out only other "bad" ones. She is the *delinquent girl*.

In adolescence she engages in a frantic search for relation with a substitute "mother" who will give her momentary confirmation that she is worthy of receiving love. She may also be aping the only group that accepts her. All of her relationships are foreclosed before they get under way, since she presupposes and anticipates infidelity in each relationship and therefore perpetually looks to the next one. Her search for relation thus compulsively goes on. Outside of relation, she feels she is a nothing. Autonomy develops only with attention and guidance from significant others and the delinquent has had no such attention. Moreover, her continual search for substitutes for the relationships that she missed leaves little time for sustained autonomous activity.

The delinquent seems self-defeatingly to flaunt the mores of her family and community while at the same time she craves their acceptance and remains within their emotional and intellectual confines. A conformist in negative garb, she has to endure a two-fold retribution imposed by her community and herself.

The parents of the girl who becomes the *anarchic bohemian* have been "present" in full force. She is not neglected or abandoned but is paid attention to only as somebody strange or peculiar. She starts out as the "good" girl, often the precocious girl, whose parents seem to confirm precocity in young children. But instead of being rewarded for this precocity, she is confirmed, and vehemently so, only as eccentric. Eventually she affirms herself as strange and different, doing what other people don't do. To be different or peculiar means to be twisted at the source (unlike the delinquent, who is "bad" but has some potentiality for becoming "good"). The only hope for adequate affirmation comes outside conventional relationship. She will spurn societal norms of stable sex life, steady work, and self-discipline and also the norms of appearance and behavior in her predominant peer group. She will live a life of sensation and spontaneity. She will search for the autonomy she never has had.

She withdraws into a bohemian subgroup and conforms to its way of life, though even here her existence is essentially solitary. Her posture of aesthetic and sometimes ethical superiority may indicate that she craves acceptance from more conventional peers but feels inferior. "If you can't confirm me for what I am," she seems to say, "then I shall affirm myself as the superior one."

At the extreme, the parents have never listened to the child, from a very early age. Even her "badness" gets little response from the mother. She is confirmed as *no* one, and she affirms herself in this manner. She has little experience either in autonomy or relation. She becomes a *mute schizophrenic.*

In Chapters Four to Nine, I shall describe in greater detail these adolescent types and shall ask about each type: How was she "confirmed" by her family and important others and how does she now "affirm" herself? What are the extent of her autonomy and the nature of her relationships?

OTHER RELEVANT STUDIES

The autonomy-relation framework for the analysis of the adolescent girl is in the tradition of Rank, Fromm, Angyal, Mac-Murray, and Buber. Angyal and Buber have already been referred to.

Otto Rank speaks about man as suffering from both the fear of life and the fear of death. The primary fear, the fear of birth and of life, is the fear of autonomy. This is the fear of the adult-oriented or the peer-oriented girl. It is the fear of having to live as an isolated individual apart, for example, from parents or peers, the fear of losing connection with the whole. The other fear, the fear of death, is the fear of too much relation and too little individuality, the fear of being dissolved into the whole.[15] This is the fear of the anarchic bohemian who flees from her family and discards all of its values.

[15] Otto Rank, *Will Therapy and Truth and Reality,* trans. Jessie Taft (New York: Alfred A. Knopf, Inc., 1950). First published in two separate volumes, 1936.

The theme of autonomy and relation pervades much of Erich Fromm's writings. He asks the question: How does man cope, in nonproductive and productive ways, with his inevitable aloneness and the consequent necessity of making his own choices? In *The Sane Society*, for example, he contrasts the illusory sense of self achieved from following the herd or from attaching oneself to a socioeconomic role with the sense of self arising from activity as a loving, thinking, feeling individual.[16] The path selected by the autonomous girl he would regard as productive, the ways of the others, nonproductive, whether through immersion in the group of adults or peers, through the unrelenting search for relationships of the delinquent, or through the flight from early relationships and the search for autonomy of the anarchic bohemian.

MacMurray's analysis can be used to characterize the autonomous girl. MacMurray speaks about personal relations with others as the "positive" and the withdrawal from personal relations as the "negative" but necessary phase in the development of the person in his relationships. The autonomous girl withdraws from relations and becomes the thinker, the observer, the spectator. Such autonomous activity is "negative" in the sense of being pure knowing without action; it "goes away" from relationships. "Without the negative," says MacMurray, "there could be no development of the positive, but only the repetition *ad infinitum* of an original undifferentiated identity." [17] The development of the "negative" (that is, autonomy) enables the girl to return and to participate in relationships of mutual respect with other free, knowing agents.

Sullivan's approach based on "reflected appraisals" can be used to characterize all types other than the autonomous girl. According to Sullivan, the child structures her behavior not in her own personal, spontaneous fashion (as does the autonomous girl), but in a manner calculated to avoid anxiety and gain security through approval from others. She early becomes sensitized to the appraisals of significant others, and the self is organized on the basis of these

---

[16] Erich Fromm, *The Sane Society* (New York: Holt, Rinehart & Winston, Inc., 1955). *See also* his *Escape from Freedom* (New York: 1941), and *Man for Himself* (New York: Holt, Rinehart & Winston, Inc., 1947).

[17] MacMurray, *Persons in Relation*, p. 91.

appraisals. For example, Sullivan characterizes a negativistic person as one whose self is organized on the basis of appraisals that make him insignificant; an incorrigible person as one whose self is organized on the basis of parental appraisals of dissatisfaction; an inadequate person as one whose integration with others is built upon dependency, arising from obedience as a child to a domineering parent or the example of a helpless parent.[18] My description of the confirmation of all adolescent types except the autonomous resembles Sullivan's developmental syndromes, although not in any one-to-one manner.

[18] Harry Stack Sullivan, *Conceptions of Modern Psychiatry* (Washington, D.C.: The William Alanson White Psychiatric Foundation, 1947), pp. 28-42.

two

THE SELECTION
OF THE
SAMPLE

If adolescence is considered to begin with early puberty and to culminate in the maturing of all personal functions
(for example, the attainment of normal heterosexual relations, independence from parents, and beginnings in the assumption of adult
responsibilities), then adolescence may extend for many years beyond high school. The sample here was arbitrarily limited to high
school (and a few junior-high school) girls.

SELECTION AND DESCRIPTION
OF THE HOSPITAL GIRLS

The girls at the hospitals belonged to different classes,
races, and religions and had been given a variety of diagnostic labels.
At the state hospitals the girls came largely from the lower or working classes and were white, Negro, and Puerto Rican, while middle-
class Jewish girls predominated at the private hospital. Most of the
girls had not suffered earlier setbacks but had come to the hospital
caught up in the maelstrom of adolescence.

One girls' ward was studied at each of two state mental hospitals.
This comprised all of the adolescent girls in the Children's Unit
at one hospital and one of seven girls' wards at the second hospital
—an experimental ward for which girls were selected who might
benefit most from a "therapeutic milieu." (Consequently the expe-

17

rience on the latter ward did not duplicate that at the first state hospital.) In addition to the 61 girls on the two wards of the state hospitals, the 18 teen-agers in the adolescent girls' pavilion of a private hospital were observed.

At the two state hospitals the girls were often socially deprived adolescents who had engaged in antisocial activity that their families and communities found intolerable.[1] Some were sexually promiscuous girls who had run away from home and school and been picked up by the police. Some had been physically aggressive against their classmates or siblings, their mothers, or their teachers. Many showed depressive features and there was some preoccupation with suicide. On the fringe were a few withdrawn schizophrenics. The girls came largely from economically deprived families, many of whom were receiving public welfare assistance. The group at the first state hospital was strongly nonwhite (19 out of 32 girls) while the second was predominantly white.[2] On the average, the girls tested at the dull normal level of intelligence, though the range of intelligence was great.

Only a small number of the girls at the private hospital came as a consequence of antisocial activity, which, when present, was usually running away or sexual promiscuity rather than physical aggression. There seemed more obsessive and compulsive symptoms among the private hospital adolescents—such as compulsive cleanliness, compulsive religiosity, obsessive ideas concerning sex, religion, and philosophy. Depressive and paranoid symptoms were seen at all the hospitals but they seemed here more often to accompany a schizophrenic pattern. There was little overt homosexuality in any

[1] A little more than half of the girls at the first state hospital were referred either directly or indirectly from a law enforcement agency. Most of the 17 girls thus referred were either picked up by the police or brought to court by their families on grounds of incorrigibility. Fewer girls came from the courts at the second state hospital.

[2] Sixteen of the 29 girls in this second group were white American, seven were Negro, and six were white Puerto Rican (that is, they or their parents were born in Puerto Rico). The white girls were usually Catholic, the nonwhite girls, usually Protestant.

The girls' parents were often immigrants. This is especially true for the nonwhite girls. Out of 15 nonwhite girls for whom data were available at the first state hospital, the fathers of 12 and the mothers of 11 were born either in the southern United States or in one of the Caribbean islands.

of the groups. Girls of above average intelligence were found more frequently at the private hospital than at the state hospitals. The girls at the private hospital came from a wide range of economic strata,[3] though most were middle class, either in family background or in personal orientation.

Half the girls in the private hospital, one-third at the second state hospital, and only one-seventh at the first state hospital had been living since birth with both parents. Among the private hospital girls, the family had been split by death, divorce, and separation. Many of the state hospital girls were born out of wedlock and had been reared in fatherless households by unwed mothers or grandmothers, or in foster homes and institutions.

SELECTION AND DESCRIPTION OF THE GIRLS IN THE COMMUNITY

The girls in the hospital sample were captive participants. Once a ward was selected, every girl was included in the sample. The girls in the community represented clusters geographically and socioeconomically, but were interviewed individually or in pairs and were not observed as a large captive group. Thirty-eight girls came from suburban high schools; 34, from city schools.

The suburban sample

The suburban sample came from five high schools. High school opinion leaders provided names of girls and these girls suggested others until the intended suburban sample size was reached. Girls were sought who were academic and commercial students, daters and nondaters, extracurricular-activity-oriented and not so oriented, serious and not so serious students. I included representatives of various races, classes, and religions. I attempted in an informal manner to cover as wide as possible a range of inter-

---

[3] The amount of payment varied with the family's ability to pay. The sources of referral were usually other hospitals, private psychiatrists, and occasionally the court. About 10 per cent of referrals were accepted. The criteria for admission that the hospital tried to maintain were: (1) a relatively good premorbid history; (2) a cooperative family; and (3) a girl with some insight and a desire for change.

ests and backgrounds. There was no attempt to select the sample in a random manner.

Most of the girls were middle class. Their fathers were at least high school graduates and were usually in the professions or in business. All families were intact except for one in which the father had died and another in which the parents had been divorced. The suburban girls paralleled the private hospital girls in most socio-economic characteristics. The girls seemed average and above in intelligence.

The city sample

The city girls came from twelve city schools and lived within one circumscribed city area. Though the sample included, at one end, girls from private schools and from the New York public High School of Music and Art, it was weighted heavily by children of lower- and working-class Negroes who lived in Harlem.[4] The girls in the city sample had an extremely wide range of intelligence and articulateness.

A sizable proportion of the lower- and working-class Negro girls came from broken families whose parents had been separated for periods of a few months to many years. Almost all the families of the middle-class girls were intact. All parents were living and no girls were reared in foster homes or institutions.

Most of the city girls resembled the state hospital girls in social and economic characteristics.

The sample of city girls was acquired from the administrative heads of two community centers, who gave names of regular attenders at the centers, infrequent visitors, and girls in the area who had never been to the centers; additional names were obtained from the girls themselves.

Through the methods described above for obtaining interviewees, I found few autonomous girls. This is probably a commentary on the scarcity of such girls. In order to investigate the autonomous

---

[4] Fewer Puerto Ricans appeared in the community sample than in the hospital sample but there were several representatives of other minority groups that were not in the hospital sample—for example, Japanese and Chinese.

type, I was led to explore other ways of seeking out such girls. I visited one large art center and contacted another. Grandmothers were there and young children of four and five but no high school girls. I called a large political club soon after national elections and the administrative official informed me that he could give me the names of "dedicated" high school boys or young married women— but no high school girls. High school girls were too involved either with their peers or with getting into college, according to these organizational informants. Their commitment would come later on. Finally, through the "dedicated" boys, I did find additional autonomous girls in the civil rights movement.

three

AUTONOMY AND RELATION
IN THREE ASPECTS
OF LIVING:
AN OVERVIEW

The nature and extent of a girl's autonomy and relation could not be studied in the abstract but had to have substantive bases.

During my initial participant observation at the private hospital
I observed that the girls were engaged in intensive self-scrutiny. In
their talk, their fights, and their fantasies they seemed to be asking,
Who am I, where did I come from, and where am I going, and they
put these questions in concrete form. For example, Do I act like a
lesbian or a normal girl? Am I Negro or African or West Indian?
Will I be wealthy and cultured? Do I want to be a wife and mother
or lead the free, rich, intellectual life? Shall I become a disciple
of Gandhi, Christ, or Martin Luther King? [1]

Such questions concerned three aspects of a girl's living. These
aspects emerged as suitable substantive foci for observation, namely,

---

[1] Erikson has employed the concept of identity as a means for studying a
person's concern with who he is. He regards identity as the relatively coherent
integration that gradually evolves out of what a person is constitutionally—his
endowment and temperament—and what he is becoming psychosocially through
significant identifications and consistent social roles. One's sense of identity
helps to bind together the past, present, and future into a coherent whole.
Though the establishment of an identity neither begins nor ends with adolescence,
but is a life-long development, the hard core of unique personality, Erikson feels,
has been established by adolescence. See Erik H. Erikson, *Childhood and Society*
(New York: W. W. Norton & Company, Inc., 1950); *see also* his *Identity and the
Life Cycle* (New York: International Universities Press, 1959).

(1) concern with body and its functions; (2) relations with peers (both male and female) and parents; and (3) experiences in matters intellectual, aesthetic, religious, and political.

These existential aspects of living are dependent on one another. For example, a girl's image of her body may be so negative that she is inhibited from meeting boys and sharing experiences with them. Or her dependence on the expectations and approval of a particular social group may be so overriding that she forecloses the possibilities for independent exploration in a larger world of the intellect and the arts and of social or political action.

The three aspects also vary somewhat independently. For example, a girl may develop self-direction and maturity in her relations among political associates without being able to establish a relationship leading to some fidelity with a boy.

The fully rounded girl is developing her autonomy and her relation simultaneously in all aspects of her living. Her development is stunted when one or more aspects of living are closed to her.

Before turning in later chapters to the way these various aspects of living are experienced by girls with differing degrees of autonomy and relation, I shall present here a generalized overview of the adolescent girl's experience.

CONCERN WITH HER BODY

During the two years preceding puberty, a girl undergoes first a spurt in physical growth, then a change in body proportions, and finally the maturing of her primary and secondary sex characteristics. These biological changes reach a climax at puberty in the menarche, the first menses.[2] The girl focuses attention on her body as a consequence of these crucial body changes and also of her desire for acceptance by her contemporaries and her anticipation of utilizing her body in relations with boys. The perception

---

[2] The menarche usually occurs between the ages of 11 and 16 among girls in the United States, with a mean menarchial age of 13.5. *See* J. R. Gallagher, "General Principles in Clinical Care of Adolescent Patients," *Pediatric Clinics of North America*. Vol. VII, No. 1 (1960). Quoted in Peter Blos, *On Adolescence* (New York: The Free Press, 1962), p. 6.

and the evaluation of her body (her body image), ever changing, are basic experiences in her life.[3]

Her image of her body and her anticipated use of her body are visualized within the framework of cultural and familial definitions of beauty and goodness.

Her mother, the mass media, and later her peers emphasize that a girl should be beautiful and they spell out the "perfect" measurements. The feminine form, they indicate, should be clothed in beauty and glamour which are irresistible to men. Beauty is largely equated with youth. (At least youth is a necessary if not a sufficient condition for beauty.) A girl's mother tries to keep her body glamorous and to conceal the ravages of age, her precarious security seeming to depend upon perpetual attractiveness.[4]

A girl sees her own body largely through the eyes of her family. If they confirm her as ugly, she "can't hear" the contradictions of her peers.

Her family emphasizes that a girl be good, equating goodness with chastity. No longer Puritanical, they may look the other way and not ask too many questions. The girl may even feel free to talk with her mother about necking or petting. But the limits are clear and distinct. She is relatively "free" to do what she wants but she cannot get pregnant. From childhood, her parents have conjured up the bogey man who might try to molest her. By adolescence, her world lets her know that she is no longer an innocent victim but a

---

[3] *See* Paul Schilder, *The Image and Appearance of the Human Body* (London: Kegan Paul Co., 1935).

[4] Our emphasis on looks and sight and deemphasis on touch fits in with the premium on youth. Margaret Mead speculates on "the lack of skin sensuousness of Americans as a group . . . , the non-sensuousness that makes looks and appearance loom so large in love and love-making. . . ." ". . . children are drawn into the dating game not by their bodies, but by their assertiveness, their desire to achieve, to succeed, to be popular. Yet the game is cast in highly sexual terms; breast and legs are emphasized . . ." (*Male and Female* [New York: William Morrow & Co. Inc., 1949], pp. 261, 288).

Robert Bell, almost 20 years later, again mentions the importance we give to "looks." "American values suggest that the American girl can be sexually *attractive* but not sexually *active*." (The italics are his.) In fact, "Most American girls are socialized to be as sexually attractive as possible as an important part of successful participation in the dating-courtship process." (*Premarital Sex in a Changing Society* [Englewood Cliffs, N.J.: Prentice-Hall, Inc., 1966], pp. 52, 165).

willing dupe. She must set rigorous limits on what she can give or she may acquire a "bad girl" reputation. The boy is "masculine" in displaying his sexual passion but she is "bad." She is the child-bearing animal created for reproduction while the boy is the predatory and pleasure-loving animal.

Within this cultural and familial context, then, it is not surprising that the girl should continually ask herself how she measures up. Is she normal in height, weight, and size of bust, in roundness of hips and body proportions? Her concern begins with body externals of hair, face, and weight—the parts that show. She washes her hair frequently, she abhors any semblance of acne, and she diets often.[5] She paints her lips or face, acquires a new coiffure and new clothes.

From her face, her concern goes to her bust. "I'm beginning to get a figure," she notes, usually pridefully. But then there is the fear: is it growing too fast? Or else, am I behind schedule? Has it stopped growing too soon?

She regards menstruation as a "curse" rather than a blessing.[6] The advantages that accrue are too far in the future. "I'm a woman, what of it," she queries. "I can't go out and get pregnant." Menstruation is a monthly reminder of cultural and biological restric-

[5] When girls are asked, in a nationwide survey, what they would like to change in themselves, more than half express the desire for some change in their looks, often in the face (*Adolescent Girls* [Ann Arbor: Survey Research Center, University of Michigan, 1957], pp. 13, 14).

Shyness, weight, and skin condition are the major problems of readers of the teen-type magazine (Charles H. Brown, "Self-Portrait: The Teen-Type Magazine," in *Teen-Age Culture, Annals of the American Academy of Political and Social Science,* CCCXXXVIII [November 1961], 13).

[6] *See* Clara Thompson, "Cultural Pressures in the Psychology of Women," in Patrick Mullahy (ed.), *A Study of Interpersonal Relations* (New York: Grove Press, Inc., orig. Hermitage Press, 1949), p. 137.

A mother sometimes feels very reluctant to talk with her daughter about menstruation and more readily talks about conception, pregnancy, and birth, according to Helene Deutsch. Her daughter, of course, observes this. (*The Psychology of Women* [New York: Grune & Stratton, Inc., 1944], Vol. I, p. 152). Hopefully, the situation has changed in the last few decades.

Margaret Mead suggests that "Careful studies of dysmenorrhea in America have failed to reveal any consistent factors among women who manifest pain except exposure during childhood to another female who reported menstrual pain" (*Male and Female,* p. 220).

tions. It interferes with her scheduled activity (for example, swimming, tennis, dancing). It's embarrassing if she starts menstruating in school. She is "afraid of blood showing, with the boys around." Moreover, it's often painful or at least disconcerting. "You don't feel like yourself, especially the first day. Everything irritates you. You want to lie around. But you can't do anything about it, that's nature," she says resignedly. "There's not one who has told me they don't get cramps. I don't think a girl should go through all that pain." She is not concerned at this stage with menstruation as a prelude to motherhood.

RELATIONS WITH GIRLS

Relations with other girls are marked by ambivalence.

On the one hand, other girls represent the familiar and the known and much of a girl's time is spent in the company of other girls. She can relax with them. She can let her hair down or put it up. A girl seeks out these others, most like herself, as companions, confidantes, and models at a time when she is not yet sure of herself. Moving toward boys, she is beset by uncertainties, and so she turns back to the familiar home ground to test her feelings and observations, ask for advice, or ventilate her grievances. "How am I doing?" she wants to know. The "telling" becomes an end in itself. "One of the great attractions of boys for girls is that they can talk to other girls about it," it is recognized.

On the other hand, she competes with other girls. Is another more popular with boys, friendlier with girls, a better dresser or dancer? she wonders. The power struggle, if it may be so called, is usually played out covertly among middle-class girls. The girl learns that the overt aggression of the bully is socially unacceptable in her middle-class group, that her aims must be achieved through stratagem and subterfuge.

She may compete with other girls for many status-laden objects but the chief object of competition is invariably the boy. The "old maid" is a worse fate than the "old bachelor" and the girl begins early to try to insure her future. One girl analyzes the situation: "In this society we're brought up so that girls seem to concentrate all their lives on boys. A girl who seems dull begins to sparkle when a boy approaches."

"You can't trust another girl" is a prevalent (but not universal) theme among high school girls. If the interviewing had been done several years earlier in the girls' lives, when they were idealizing other girls rather than boys, such nontrusting attitudes probably would not have appeared.

The statements below are made by a variety of girls, some typed as peer-oriented, some adult-oriented, and some autonomous.

It's hard to find a true friend.

As long as there isn't a boy involved, two girls can be close friends. As soon as one gets an advantage of any sort over the other, the lower one will try to slit the other's throat.

Girls get along well until they become rivals—maybe about clothes and looks but mostly about boys.

I don't feel that I can trust most of my girl friends a lot of the time. They talk.

People can trust me, but that's all I'll count on.

A girl can go just so far in a friendship. She does things as though she is helping another girl but instead she may mess up a relation with a boy.

More sympathetically, it is noted: "You can grow out of a friend. You may need her in a certain period or she may need you. Whenever one grows out of the friendship first, it's painful for the other."

A teen-age boy is regarded as more scrupulous and trustworthy than a girl, at least until he is in his twenties and considers marriage. A boy may be "catty" about girls but he is being playful, the girls feel. A girl, on the other hand, expresses violently antagonistic feelings toward other girls.

Thus, though the high school girl looks for guidance or confirmation among her female peers and for relations with girls as an end in itself, a camouflaged wariness toward other girls often persists.[7]

[7] That loyalty to personal friends is usually subordinated to other values is found by Havighurst and Taba in their study of 16-year-olds in a small midwestern community (Hilda Taba, "Moral Beliefs and the Ability to Apply Them in Solving Problems of Conduct," in Robert J. Havighurst and Hilda Taba,

RELATIONS WITH BOYS

In her early adolescent years, a girl often engages in romantic fantasy, with photographs of crooners and movie actors—inaccessible, distant idols—plastered on the walls of her bedroom. Gradually she participates in relations with boys of her acquaintance.

Almost all girls want to date. The excitement over dating is partly the excitement of the "game," the game of getting and keeping a boy until another one appears. Emphasis is placed on the frequency of dating. "Girls want to date a lot," one girl evaluates. "It doesn't really matter whether it's the same person." On the other hand, to date a "big wheel" is a singular accomplishment. A girl takes less risk in this game if she can be the decision-maker, especially when the decision means the termination of the relationship. "She is upset if a boy breaks up. Her pride is involved."

The excitement over boys is also the excitement of "play" as an end in itself. This "play" involves talk, such "kicks" as can be had through dancing, movies, riding around, listening to music, and some sexual adventure. It is not the play for relief of tension or for relaxation that the adult may experience but rather it is the play of experimentation in emerging heterosexuality. This play is serious and essential for the girl. The banter with boys, the dancing, and the riding around are not mere frivolity but the beginnings of trial-and-error relationships. Many such relationships end up on the side of error, but can be important learning experiences nonetheless.

Sexual experimentation is of greater importance than other aspects of play and so arouses more fear of the unknown and greater fear of failure. It is not surprising, then, that the sexual act is enshrouded in a maze of contradictions for the high school girl. It is the "greatest" thing in the world but it is also "bad" and "painful." The experience is reputed to be either highly exhilarating or tediously boring. It is alluded to in dress and manner and in exuberant fantasy although there is little discussion in specific terms. The frequency of sex talk, together with its generality, lends excitement and mystery and the girl is often disenchanted by the reality ex-

Adolescent Character and Personality [New York: John Wiley & Sons, Inc., 1949], pp. 81-96).

perience. "It's built up and so talked about that you think it's the greatest thing in the world. It's pretty disappointing," one girl concedes. "Boys have more fun out of it. They're the ones who start it." "A girl always keeps in mind that she shouldn't get aroused, but I don't think she really does get aroused." "She might get used to it, though, and get to like it."

If she doesn't find sexual intimacies pleasurable, she is apprehensive that she's not quite a woman. "Is something wrong with me that I get bored from necking?" she wonders. "That I don't want to go all the way? Why don't I feel anything? Am I incapable of feeling?"

In general, she necks and pets but goes no further. Petting serves as a stop-gap measure that defines the limits of social acceptability and conceals any fear of sexual relationships.[8]

APPROVAL FROM PEERS

A girl finds it essential to her sense of well-being to be approved by the peers of her choice. She needs this basis of security to make further forays into the new territory of dating and sexual experimentation, or of intellectual, aesthetic, and political involve-

---

[8] The increase in teen-age sexual behavior over the last generation has been in the area of petting and in the public nature of petting behavior, according to Ira L. Reiss, "Sexual Codes in Teen-Age Culture," *Annals of the American Academy of Political and Social Science*, CCCXXXVIII (November 1961), 59.

According to Reiss, "the vast majority of our approximately twenty million teen-agers are not only not extreme but are quite conservative and restrained in the area of premarital sexual codes and behavior when we compare them to their older brothers and sisters" (*Ibid*, p. 60).

Bell summarizes our present research information about premarital sexual values and behavior. ". . . Since approximately the time of World War I," he says, "there is no strong evidence that the rates of premarital coitus have been increasing. Therefore, the belief that premarital sexual experience is much more common, especially for girls, since the end of World War II is not supported by available research evidence." He adds elsewhere that "For the female, premarital coitus usually depends on strong emotional commitment and plans for marriage. The Terman, Burgess and Wallin, and Kinsey studies found that from half to two-thirds of the females in their studies reported premarital coitus only with the men they eventually married." (Robert Bell, *Premarital Sex in a Changing Society*, pp. 12, 58.)

ments. The more strange and unknown the new territory, the more she is dependent upon her home base for emotional security.

She becomes increasingly aware of how she differs from peers in her family, class, religion, and race; and in her sexual, social, and intellectual development. She is Negro or Catholic or Jewish or Puerto Rican or foreign-born; or she has a hooked nose or crooked teeth or large hips or small breasts; she is good or bad; or she is too smart or too dumb. She becomes increasingly self-conscious about many experiences—for example, walking alone with a boy; exposing intellectual weakness or strength in the classroom; or joining her peers when she senses ostracism because of her minority group status or her bad-girl reputation.

She is aware of who is "in" and who is "out" among her peers. The "outs" are girls who deviate from peer group norms, don't share group interests and values, or stand out in some way as peculiar. The more extreme among them are sometimes labeled "creeps" or "fags," labels that have no necessary homosexual connotation. The "out" may be a serious girl in a boisterous group; a nonintellectual in a group of would-be intellectuals; a girl who is maturing physically and socially more slowly than her peers or one who communicates only with adults. The girl may stand out as different by virtue of her color, religion, class, mannerisms, or physical attributes, and hence be regarded as beyond the pale by her favored peers.

A girl often engages in activity that helps to put her "in." Her interest in sports, for example, is often determined by what gives prestige in her school. Basketball and volleyball add status in some schools; in other schools, all sports are "necessary evils." Being a cheerleader or twirler often gives validation that she is "in." The cheerleader works with the athletes to lead the school to victory and shares their popularity. In addition, the cheerleader has the thrill provided by being on public display. The cheerleaders often form an elite group that is highly selective in membership.

Participation in dramatics, too, can provide elite status as well as the thrill of being on public display. A girl may see her interest in dramatics as a passing phase. "I don't want to be an actress. I don't think I could stand the life," she says. "Now, it's more a means to express myself. Since I haven't got my ideas straight, I like to express myself a lot. It's part of my adolescence. After marriage, it won't mean the same thing it does now."

Sometimes a girl engages in activity that results in putting her "out." In some manner this girl has already been dealt out of the in-group. In her effort to get into an out-group she may start truanting or run away with a boy and thus remove herself further from the in-group. "I didn't want to get in anyway," she says in sour-grapes fashion. She finalizes the process by declaring, "You [the in-group] are the fags and the squares."

Getting "in" with peers may be beyond a girl's control. The middle-class Negro girl, for example, has no in-group unless she comes from a large city school. Although she exudes good taste, holds school office, and gets good grades, she is not wholly "in." "Kids try to be nice but you can sense," says a Negro girl. "The majority [of white girls] don't hate Negroes, they're afraid of them. Their parents drive into them about Negroes." "In school you'll be very good friends but beyond that usually you can't make it unless they go against their parents' wishes." A white girl corroborates this view: "We don't visit in each others' houses. There are rarely invitations extended either way." "There's a great deal of prejudice. At lunch, you can see the Negro table. If the white girls truly believed their religion, you wouldn't see this. It must come from the home. It starts in the sixth to eighth grade."

Such a girl without an in-group may affirm herself as genuine, in autonomous fashion, but get no such confirmation from her peers. This marginal girl is forced, if she is to remain genuine, to seek out those persons who will respect her, who will confirm her as a genuine person.

EXPERIENCES IN INTELLECTUAL, AESTHETIC, POLITICAL, OR RELIGIOUS MATTERS

The adolescent, according to Piaget, has reached a new juncture in her intellectual development. Between the ages of eleven and fourteen, the capacity for abstract thought becomes realized. She can not only think but can think about her previous thought and she can envisage all possible potentialities.[9] She can also act upon her knowledge. She can thus expand to a new limit her insight and foresight in intellectual, aesthetic, or political and religious pursuits and in the relations that accompany her pursuits. How much each type of adolescent girl fulfills such potentialities will be discussed in the chapters that follow.

In summary, in looking at the different types of girls, I use as my framework the concepts of confirmation and affirmation, and of autonomy and relation in the various aspects of living; and I use the following format as a context for my exposition of this conceptual framework: (1) a girl's confirmation by her parents; (2) a girl's mode of affirmation, (a) how much investment in autonomy; (b) concern with her body and its functions; (c) relations with peers; (d) intellectual, aesthetic, or political concerns; religious involvement; marriage or career.

I shall attempt to show that only the autonomous girl affirms herself in a manner that portends emotional maturity in adulthood. She has a strong sense of the "I" of autonomy (*I* think, *I* feel, *I* participate) and her relations with others are beginning to extend beyond reciprocity and to encompass a more personal and intimate encounter. I shall indicate the kind of confirmation the autonomous girl received from her family (as compared with other girls) that led to such positive beginnings in autonomy and personal relation.

[9] *See* Bärbel Inhelder and Jean Piaget, *The Growth of Logical Thinking from Childhood to Adolescence* (New York: Basic Books, Inc., Publishers, 1958); *see also* John H. Flavell, *The Developmental Psychology of Jean Piaget* (Princeton: D. Van Nostrand Co. Inc., 1963), pp. 202-225, 415.

four

THE
PEER-ORIENTED
GIRL

The peer-oriented girl, having had too little relation
with her parents, "loses herself" compensatorily in her relations with
peers. She has been confirmed by her parents in certain of her external aspects—as "pretty" or "fun-loving" or "high class" or "popular"
—and she continues thus to affirm herself in her relations with her
peers. These externals become the goals or ends of her living and all
else becomes means to achieve these ends.

Within prescribed limits set by her adult and her peer culture,
she has had some freedom to experiment and to develop positive
relationships with girls and boys. However, such freedom has been
limited by her restrictive confirmation in externals. She enters a
relation desirous of pleasing others, submitting to others, or having
power over others, but she is not independently self-assertive.[1] She
may be able to establish a reciprocal relationship with others—
giving "this for that"—but she has little experience in relationships
based on intimacy and love.

[1] The peer-oriented girl's outlook resembles the marketing orientation described by Erich Fromm in *Man For Himself* (New York: Holt, Rinehart &
Winston, Inc., 1947). *See also* the other-directed mode of conformity postulated
by David Riesman in *The Lonely Crowd*, in collaboration with Reuel Denney
and Nathan Glazer (New Haven: Yale University Press, 1950), and in *Faces in
the Crowd*, in collaboration with Nathan Glazer (New Haven: Yale University
Press, 1952).

Too little relation with mother

The peer-oriented girl generally says that she loves her
mother. But she doesn't confide in her. Her confidantes belong to
her own generation. "You depend more on your friends. I confide in
my older sister or older brother or in girl friends." "I write in my
diary."

A ban on communication between mother and daughter covers
what the girl regards as most personal: the functioning of her sexual
organs, her relations with boys, the confidences of girl friends, and
the termination of friendships with girls. The generational gap
always intrudes. "We talk more in generalities, not in great detail. I
explain my English composition to her." The mother seems to fear
the discussion of any intimacies. The daughter, in turn, hesitates to
introduce apparently taboo topics to her mother. "I'd feel funny
talking to my mother about sex," she confesses. Yet she points her
finger accusingly, "Why didn't my mother tell me the facts of life?"
And her only consolation is that "most mothers don't really sit down
and explain sex or anything like that. By the time they're ready,
you've already heard it."

If the older generation expresses interests that are similar to hers,
so much the worse for them. The enthusiasm for the avant garde
among her elders isn't "natural," she feels. Those of her elders who
produce avant garde literature aren't writing for their own generation but for hers. "Older people can be 'cool,' but it's never the
same thing," she maintains.

She complains that her mother is too preoccupied with her own
living and neglects her. "She goes to work and doesn't have time. I
couldn't get close to her." "She drinks a lot. She goes out with men,
running in and out, and leaves me stuck with the brats. She has too
many children."

[2] No data are available on how the girl actually was confirmed by her parents
from her earliest years. I am inferring that her present relationship with parents
is suggestive of her earlier confirmation.

All the data for the peer-oriented, the adult-oriented, and the autonomous types were taken from the interview material on the girls *outside* the
hospital in the community.

A girl's own generation "knows best" and so she is critical of parental controls. "She doesn't let me do what everybody else does. I'd let my children do more, stay out later. My mother thinks she's still back in her old days." She is disdainful of her mother's gratuitous advice. Her mother may tell her how to act with boys: "Don't be athletic" or "Act more feminine." The girl feels that she already knows more about such matters than her mother. Or "She thinks she knows the right way about cultural things," the girl says with bemused tolerance of her mother's attempts to impart knowledge. "She's a sweet old soul, though, no matter what I say."

Despite the mutual withdrawal, her mother has been a model to her, the peer-oriented girl thinks, even more when she was younger than at present. In describing her mother as a model, the daughter gives some indication of how she, the daughter, was confirmed from her earliest years and how she hopes to affirm herself. Her mother is "well mannered and well dressed, shows you how to eat, tells you about swearing, keeps the house right, is happy. She goes out, she has fun." The mother may not always fit this peer-oriented ideal. Sometimes "she dresses wrong and looks sloppy. I see her in the most unromantic situations: mowing the lawn, taking out the garbage, her hair up in curlers, and I see her acting silly with her friends. She might be trying to impress other adults." The discussion about mother as a model is concerned with such "externals" as dress, coiffure, and manners.

Too little relation with father

A girl's father provides her first contact with a man. She gets through him her initial experience of what men are like and what she might look for among her peers.[3]

---

[3] The girl's presumed devotion to her father is interpreted sexually by Freud. According to Freud, a girl's original love object is her mother, but when she discovers her own and her mother's castration, she turns from mother to father. The mother, who receives from father what the girl herself wants, becomes her rival. (Sigmund Freud, "The Psychology of Women," in *New Introductory Lectures on Psycho-analysis* [New York: W. W. Norton & Company, Inc., 1933], pp. 153-185.)

Simone de Beauvoir stresses not the sexual but the transcendental daughter-father experience. The father, though not authoritative in daily household affairs, actually reigns supreme in the daughter's eyes. On all important issues the mother demands, rewards, and punishes in his name and through his

There seems to be a mutually reinforced lack of attention between father and daughter among peer-oriented girls. "My father lives here and I hardly ever talk to him," a girl confesses. "I don't really pay much attention to him. He's away so much and when he's home he reads the paper or sleeps most of the evening." He shows concern only when she goes out at night, a lower-class girl complains, and then he is frightened that something will happen, "as if I don't know what to do. I tell him that I'm not that kind of girl but he doesn't know for sure. Maybe he has to support the baby or something. He has the responsibility."

Even when the father is referred to favorably, there is no indication that the father-daughter relationship is close. "He keeps his word. He's interested in my best." "He's good-natured and friendly." "I don't get punished as much by him." "I have respect for him but fathers seem more old-fashioned than mothers. Maybe because they're just not around the home so much." "I respect him. I look up to him as the head of the household, the breadwinner" (though her mother works).

The peer-oriented girl, then, seems to have had too little relation with her parents. As a substitute, she hangs on to the relation with her peers.

HER MODE OF AFFIRMATION—LITTLE INVESTMENT IN AUTONOMY

The peer-oriented girl expresses doubt about some of the beliefs and convictions of her family and other authorities but

---

authority. He incarnates for his daughter the world of adventure outside the home. The son thinks of his father's supremacy with a feeling of rivalry, but the daughter, with idolatrous admiration, passively awaits his approval. She feels fulfilled if he rewards her with affection. If he withholds his love, she feels condemned. She may then look elsewhere, becoming indifferent and even hostile toward him. It is the oldest daughter, especially the first-born, without initial sibling competitors, who is ardently attached to her father. De Beauvoir roams through history, literature, and legend to illustrate this perceived superiority of the male. (*The Second Sex,* trans. H. M. Parshley [New York: Alfred A. Knopf, Inc., 1953], pp. 287 ff.)

This transcendent devotion is not usually the picture we get of the father-daughter relationship.

she does not openly question her peers and stand alone on any major issues. She affirms herself with them as she has been confirmed by her parents in some partial, external aspect which others can readily see; for example, she is pretty and popular, she talks well, or she is always having fun. Such externals now receive the necessary additional confirmation from esteemed peers. This confirmation from peers is all-important. (Her parents' values may be similar to her peers', but it is to her peers and not her parents that she now looks for confirmation.) Her peers provide the specific content of her confirmation-affirmation process. To leave peers physically and psychologically and carry out activities independently requires greater security with peers than a girl derives from confirmation only as pretty or fun-loving. She continually needs others around her to confirm her in these externals.

The dicta of her esteemed peers cover many aspects of her living; for example, some of her feelings about her own body, how far she goes in her sex relations, her attitudes toward the academic life and toward marriage and family. She doesn't transcend group standards or exercise independent reflection and choice on any of these matters but leaves her peers only in a very superficial sense. If something happened and she didn't get the lead in the class play, one thinking peer-oriented girl muses, would she then withdraw from the peer rat race and be "herself?" "But," she says, "Like Marquand's hero in *Point of No Return,* I do get the lead," seeming to disallow the very question she has raised, as though even the thought of functioning without the support of the group is intolerable.

HER AFFIRMATION OF THE "EXTERNALS"

It is more what you make of yourself than what your parents make of you, the peer-oriented girl is saying, but what you make of yourself in limited and superficial fashion.

In describing the prerequisites of "higher class," she gives some indication of her own affirmation of such externals as knowing how to talk, to act, and to dress. "The upper-class girl isn't running around acting like she doesn't have any sense. She's not overloud. She knows what to do when she's in a group gathering—for instance if a boy asks her to dance. Some girls start giggling and are sorry afterwards. She's neat and not fancy. She's always well-groomed."

The talk, actions, and dress of the "lower-class" girl are described in unsparing and contemptuous detail. "She says ain't, double negatives, and words that come out of the gutter. She makes herself conspicuous by being loud and tough. She wears shabby sweaters and blouses with a stain, her skirts are ripped and her hair is messy. She wears bad color combinations—different plaids or plaid and print. She talks and acts and dresses like this to get attention because she feels inferior."

In this fashion the peer-oriented girl stresses proper grooming and knowing how to talk and to act as the only and sufficient prerequisites of "higher class." "Wealth doesn't phase me any more," one middle-class girl admits. "With parents so wealthy, some girls are no different from girls dragged out of the gutter. The important questions are: Does she carry herself like a lady? Is she perfectly groomed? Can she open her mouth in public?" "I don't think what a girl's father does has that much influence," asserts another middle-class girl. "Your personality is more important." And a third, "An interest in culture is not important. Girls aren't generally interested."

The peer-oriented girl summarizes her own "external" values in her description of the Beatniks.

They're odd. The clothes they wear, the long hair.

They're dirty—they don't take baths.

They dress sloppy. They have their own way of thinking in politics and dress.

They're nice—they wear different things. Real neat.

It's disgusting, the way they live.

They're not normal. They sit around and recite poetry.

Some peer-oriented girls are concerned with studies or with being "intellectual," not as an end in itself but for the social and psychological advantages that may accrue. "Class" is seen as partially at least a function of "intellectuality." Self-confidence too is viewed as a function of "intellectuality." "Most of the intellectual kids consider themselves on a higher plane. They think themselves higher class, think they have more, they have confidence in themselves," a girl explains. She would like to be included among those who "are members of the honor society, like to study more, don't get in trouble with the teachers, and win the awards at graduation." Moreover, "Girls try to get good grades," she adds. "They have college in mind." [4]

While recognizing a positive correlation between "class" and intellectuality, she feels there may be a slight negative correlation between popularity with boys and intellectuality. At best, intellectual standing is of itself no deterrent to popularity. "Nobody seems to worry much about that. Sometimes, but not too much. Boys are afraid of somebody smarter but after they get to know you, it's OK." "Being smart is not that important. It doesn't hinder you at all unless you brag about it. Girls don't try to hide it but maybe to act a little less smart than him."

Thus, intellectuality is always a means and never an end to the peer-oriented girl. It "works" with "class" but not so much with popularity.

HAVING FUN VERSUS BEING PRUDENT

The peer-oriented girl adopts the symbols of "togetherness" or defiance that her group expresses:—smoking, drinking, staying out late at night, secrecy about many trivial encounters, the jargon, the dress, the hair-do.

Her outlook is dominated by a fun ethos. She would like always to be going places, acting "daring, zany and wild," and seeming always to be having a good time.

---

[4] James Coleman indicates that when a girl is forced to choose between being remembered as a brilliant student, a leader in activities, and most popular, she is more likely to choose the image of activities leader or most popular than the brilliant student image. There is a period in the sophomore and junior years when good grades among girls are particularly deemphasized—presumably related to the beginning of regular dating. Coleman points out that "good grades" and concentration upon studies are seen by the adolescent community as acquiescence to adult constraints. Boys beginning to feel their oats are not likely to seek out girls who wholeheartedly accept adult demands. (*The Adolescent Society* [New York: The Free Press, 1961], pp. 30, 169, 172.)

Among the girls sampled here (of all types) "good grades" of themselves do not appear to have a strong negative connotation unless they are found in (1) the braggart, (2) the dull "grind," or (3) the girl who is carelessly groomed.

She takes chances, "just for kicks," on doing the proscribed—for example, smoking or drinking under age. "Lots of girls drink," she acknowledges. "More girls than boys seem to smoke." Though many of the popular girls drink and smoke, "they're not cheap," it is emphasized. Through drinking excessively, a girl may lose her good reputation but to drink moderately is to conform. "You have to conform or you feel like an outsider," she explains. "So you take chances on smoking or drinking under age. Sometimes a girl even tries marijuana. You do it because the rest do it and not because deep down inside you feel you must." One teen-age outsider (with respect to drinking) expresses indignation: "I was brought up with a real respect for the law. If you're under age, you don't drink. They think I'm nuts. 'Maybe we should abstain because it's dangerous, but illegality is no reason,' they say."

CONCERN WITH HER BODY;
HER RELATIONS WITH BOYS

The peer-oriented girl seems to anticipate using her body either directly or indirectly to add pleasure and zest to her living.

When she indicates any reluctance to disrobe in front of others, her main emphasis is not on innate modesty (as with the adult-oriented girl) but on the anticipated comparison of her body, and especially her bust, with her peers. "Your bust is different, it's smaller, not as well developed as others. Somebody else might have more and might make fun of you. Or if you do have a lot, you might feel funny about it. Unless you have a beautiful body you don't want to exhibit any inferiority."[5]

[5] Some of the peer-oriented girls who live in the city, where sexual talk and sexual activity are more prevalent among adolescent girls, indicate apprehension about the vagina, especially during the menstrual period. "Some girls come to school smelling like fish. They say that they can't take a bath. It has to be clean. If you start menstruating and then start smelling, it's very embarrassing." Moreover, "You're afraid something will happen to your private parts. You might not get any more thrills. The first thing that a girl wraps around after a shower is her bottom." The remarks quoted were made by lower-class girls.

The beginnings of menstruation are happily anticipated. Menstruation is a badge of womanhood, a sign of potential motherhood, and the peer-oriented girl often expresses pride. "This is great, I'm so old. I'm grown-up." "I didn't start until fourteen and I was worried that something was wrong." Later on, though, she finds menstruation as burdensome as do other types of adolescent girls.

Like most adolescent girls, the peer-oriented girl usually wants to go with boys more steadily than steady. "Going steady" for her precludes fun. "I wouldn't want to go steady. It's like a status symbol but it's really just tying you down," says an upper-middle-class girl determinedly. "Tied to one boy, you brood: He wants me to sit home. Is he going out? Will he discover if I go out?" A lower-class girl gives substantially the same response. "You get too serious. You get tired of the same thing. It's fun to go out with lots of boys. One boy after another, maybe two at a time, but then they'd get beat up by the second boy." The peer-oriented girl who insists she wants to go steady seems to mean "steadily." She has dated many boys but she wants to be sure of a date at the required times. "It's someone to depend on to go out with. If he doesn't appeal to you, you break off and go with another," says a girl who, at fifteen, has "gone steady" with six or seven boys.

The peer group is the referent in determining how far she goes in sexual relations. "It all depends on what everybody else is doing around you," one private-school junior maintains. "A girl may find out her friends do it so she wants to try it too," one lower-class Negro girl substantiates.

The range of sexual activity covers the gamut.

"Girls kiss but not much petting. Most boys try to go further but they'll settle for less," says a girl in a Catholic high school. "Girls kiss and pet," explains a middle-class suburbanite. "Some go all the way," says a Negro girl from Harlem.

If she goes "too far" in sexual activity, she fears primarily the rejection of her peers. "It'll get around and she'll get a bad reputation or be rushed." "Kids gossip. The boy might gossip and everybody will think. . . ." "A boy tries to make out but he won't take the responsibility of starting somebody on something like that. The girl is blamed since she can stop it." Even though the group may not condemn her openly, there is talk and snickering behind her back. "You can't help wagging tongues," she explains.[6]

The girl who has sexual intercourse asserts that she is not rejected by her peers because of this but her assertion is mixed with misgivings. "A girl isn't rejected because she does it. If she does it with one boy after another, she's rejected. If you're going together for a long time, it's taken for granted," declares one daughter of working-class parents, who then adds scornfully, "It's always a boy's fault, yet he's the one who rejects you." "You're not looked down upon by friends, just old folks," says a lower-class girl about unmarried motherhood. "Nowadays, 'she's pregnant' is as common as the saying, 'she goes to church every Sunday.' I don't think she's looked down upon unless she goes and does it with every boy," she concludes and adds her postscript, "She's looked down upon by girls, not by boys."

How pleasurable does she find her sexual experience? The sexual initiate is often dramatic in her discussion (described below) but her responses do not differ substantially from those of the girl whose sexual activity is limited to necking or petting.

Sometimes she experiences a genuine feeling of pleasure at "letting herself go." "It's an act of emotion," she explains and recounts the excitement and the thrill at letting a boy see her body. This is worth any anticipatory pain or despairing postmortems, she feels. "He gets you so hot. Once you get started you can't stop, you get carried away. He makes you feel like a woman."

Often she seems to describe a master-slave relationship that develops out of her effort to "keep" the boy or to prove her femininity and desirability. "You're just too weak, you're scared the only way

[6] C. Wayne Gordon found rigid peer group controls over sexual activity in his study, *The Social System of the High School* (New York: The Free Press, 1957), pp. 122 ff. He says that "a few of the younger girls who had been 'had at' by some of the faster, older boys had the lowest status among both boys and girls. . . . Girls known as rule breakers were ostracized by other girls. . . . a double standard for members of high and low status seemed to exist among both boys and girls." Gordon sampled 576 students of a suburban high school in a midwestern metropolitan community.

According to Coleman, too, "The girl who is too free with herself, whatever her social background, is excluded—first by the girls, with the boys concurring" (*The Adolescent Society*, p. 121).

to keep the boy is to have sex. You get mixed up with a fellow who leads you on." "You want assurance you might be desirable, that somebody will want you." She senses that she is often the dupe of the boy who taunts her with not being "natural" and goads her on with "You mean so much to me." The apocryphal story makes the rounds that the girl cries in anguish after the act is over, feels "cheapened" and wishes that she had never done it. The boy assures her he will take care of her, then gaily bids her good-bye.

With the uncertainty surrounding the sexual experience and with the group taboo on "going too far," it is not surprising that a web of secrecy pervades the sexual realm among peer-oriented girls who are middle-class. A girl may not confide even in her close friends. "I don't really think the group finds out too much unless the girl has to get married," it is conceded. "You don't usually discuss it in groups. If it's the first time for the girl, she may confide, she lets it get out of hand." A girl may brag and speak in generalities so that others assume that something "exciting" is happening, but she rarely provides details. She may want to convey the impression by the quantity of her make-up and her tight clothes that she is "easy and wild"—that she is taking risks and enjoying the consequences. This is no necessary indication of sexual indulgence, according to group consensus, but rather, a means of getting a boy's attention. "She may talk like a tramp but be a prude who is afraid to let a boy touch her and is afraid that others will find out."

The lower-class peer-oriented girl seeks confidantes among her peers on matters of sex more often than the middle-class girl. Her attitude seems fatalistic as she describes "no exit" between the man and the pill. Only "babies" seem certain. Her more frequent abandon with a boy and her failure to use contraceptives inevitably raise the possibility of pregnancy and her fears about possible family reprisals are poured out on her best girl friends. She associates contraceptives primarily with the boy wearing something and she depends upon him to "protect" her, though she is aware of his reluctance. She may douche after intercourse but is skeptical about its effectiveness and wary of its possible dangers. "Everything pushes up that way. It may stay up," she feels. "The black pill is no guarantee. It would ruin you anyway." She has heard that a girl can get something to wear and it is rumored that one neighborhood drug store sells this article without a prescription. But she knows well that "when the time comes you forget about it. Your mind is so wrapped up. You never know when it happens." If she becomes pregnant, she does not experience the same social pressure to give up her illegitimate baby as the girl of the middle class. (Her family may have been outwardly disapproving or even indignant. "Don't you bother to come home if you have a baby. I'm not going to bring the child up," they say. But they may have given earlier subtle permission.) She does not usually try to abort. She may take the "magical" pills she hears about but then she stops. "You can be messed up for the rest of your life," one girl says. "There's no sense. There's no actual shame. You see so many girls with their babies."

Is the peer-oriented girl progressing toward intimacy and love with a man? She has much in her favor: her peer culture's emphasis on continual "circulation" of the popular, on "daring" new experience, on freedom "up to a point" in sex relations, on the necessity for a body-in-use and not a body lying dormant or repudiated. On the negative side is the determination of her activity not by what she is ready for but by what her peers or a boy dictate. She is unable to confront a boy with independence and self-assertion, with a strong sense of "I want." Convinced that she is a person not worth loving in her own right, but rather for what she gives, she cannot proceed at her own pace but only at that of the boy or the group.

"IN" WITH THE GROUP?

The peer-oriented girl places great stress on who is "in" with the group and who is "out," according to peer consensus. If a girl does not talk, dress, and act well, she is "different" and consequently "out." The peer-oriented girl spells out her difference in painstaking detail (see pages 39-41).

By virtue of her color alone, the Negro girl is "out" even though her speech and dress meet peer standards. The peer-oriented girl usually imposes upon the Negro girl the stereotype of lower-class defiance and thus cuts off any personal relationship with her. "The Negro girls in our school are very wise, they're very fresh. They'll all be clowning and singing in the girls' room. They try to make themselves stand out," asserts a lower-middle-class white girl who has ample opportunity to see other varieties of behavior among Negro girls in her suburban high school. "They try to stay 'superior' and don't try to intermingle. Usually these are from poorer families," says another middle-class girl from the same school.

The peer-oriented girl who is Negro accepts the verdict of the white majority. "The Negroes, they don't care about anything. All they worry about is clothes. But the Jews save their money to go to college. And that's why they get the best opportunities." She regards a white boy who seeks her out as "mixed up." (Conceivably a girl whose friends are all Black Muslims would not accept the judgment of the white majority. However, among the peer-oriented girls who were interviewed, the reaction to the Black Muslims was almost universally negative: "They ruin our reputation—cursing, breaking up people's stores. They make us look bad." "They fight a cause that's not worth anything. White people and colored people should be together." "Africans don't consider themselves Negro. They say Negroes are ignorant and they feel superior." "I come from no Africa, I come from New York City and my hair is straight.") [7]

The Negro girl accepts the stereotype of the Negro and she also expresses resentment: "White people, they think they're too clean and too good for Negroes." "White girls try to take over our school and boss us." Adults are the real culprits, she maintains. "The parents, more than the children, are prejudiced." "I have a lot of white teachers who don't like me for no reason at all."

The peer-oriented girl of whatever color thus excludes from potential personal relation those with specified external characteristics.

INTELLECTUAL, AESTHETIC, OR POLITICAL CONCERNS; RELIGIOUS INVOLVEMENT

The peer-oriented high school girl is not searching for intellectual or aesthetic commitment. She is usually not dedicated to learning though she may study diligently, read "what's required,"

---

[7] Girls of other types respond in similar vein.

and get good grades. In high school a girl should appear to be having fun and this requires intensive work itself. Moreover, she sees little continuity between her school work and the life she has mapped out for herself.

She may parrot a little bit of philosophy and psychology and talk about music, art, and literature but she shows little conviction in any of this. "Girls aren't interested in art and music—in culture. Your personality is more important," she maintains. In her leisure, if she reads at all, she (if middle-class) picks up "not the deep symbolic books but nice romantic stories and adventures" that amuse without penetrating deeply. If she is a lower-class girl, her reading material usually consists of movie or love magazines, comic books, pocket books, or nothing at all.

She resists any deep emotional involvement in literature. "I'm not a father, how could I feel for him?" or, "What am I supposed to do, cry?" is her typical reaction to the suggestion that she try to empathize with a fictional character. She is saying, "Don't tamper with my smooth, well-running world. Don't give me ideas that will depress me. I'm only a teen-ager, what am I supposed to feel?"

She accepts without question her parents' political affiliation and expresses little interest of her own. "I'm too lazy to read the news every day," she says. "Maybe when I have more to say, I'll feel more interested."

She doesn't try to establish any relationship of mutuality or trust beyond her face-to-face groups. When she is asked specific questions about the Peace Corps or the civil rights movement, she is often either ignorant of the organizations or indifferent to their goals. "What's in it for me?" seems to be her standard for appraisal. "You can really get a feeling you're doing something for people who need help" is a remark that is rarely heard among the peer-oriented girls. More likely she confesses, "I'm not that dedicated to people that I'd be willing to give up the comforts of home." "I would want it if I'm not working steadily. It's a job." "Maybe if I'm not married and I'm bored, I could find a guy there."

Whether white or Negro, she has no desire to take part in the civil rights movement.[8] A girl could be injured, she claims defen-

---

[8] More adult-oriented than peer-oriented girls are active in the civil rights movement, though a small minority among both types.

sively, or killed or get put in jail. She has no such courage or commitment. Moreover, "If people don't like me places, I don't go," one Negro girl says resignedly. If the peer-oriented girl, whether white or Negro, is reminded of racial strife that is occurring at the time of the interview, she demurs: "I don't know." "I don't remember." "I haven't felt."

When she does express a desire to participate in political action, her motivation seems random and superficial. "I might want to do something. Something off-beat always appeals to me. It's a great disadvantage having no problem. How do you know until you've really met the problem?"

Most of the peer-oriented girls don't go to church regularly. Those who attend usually go alone, with friends, or with siblings. They give little indication that religion is crucial to their living.

The peer-oriented girl appears to be searching for a mother figure who will give solace and permit catharsis. "God is comforting —my own personal friend, always listening. He knows exactly how I feel. I don't have to tell Him." "You can tell Him your problems. He will understand if nobody else will. I have a problem at home or at school. I'm going to get in trouble, should I do it?"

The God of the peer-oriented girl intervenes in her behalf if she prays to Him. What can he do for me? she wants to know. "I was saying, please let everyone be all right and I know I wasn't just saying it to myself but to Somebody." "I'm going to have a test, God helps me. Or a dance. I hope it's going to turn out all right." "Seems like when I pray for something it comes true—that I don't get in trouble in school or that a boy likes me." Or, "I pray and He doesn't help when I need Him most—that my mother and father come together and small things too. But I just know He's there."

Her God sits in judgment and may reward or punish. "If you do something wrong, He lets you know you're wrong by letting something happen. You ask Him for forgiveness. But first you must accept Him."

To one peer-oriented girl, God is "a handsome man who never grows old."

Religion does not provide the peer-oriented girl with any sense of moral commitment, any rules to live by in her relations with others.

MARRIAGE OR CAREER

The peer-oriented girl circumscribes her future. She knows what she wants short-range. She does not envision goals that extend beyond the next five or ten years, during which time she hopes to entice a man, marry, and settle down for life.

Going to college means to her (1) having fun, (2) liberating herself from family, and (3) meeting a mate. Nothing is mentioned directly about education or career. "I'll go to college to find a husband," she confesses. "If I don't find one, I'll have something else. I can live with people of my own age and intelligence. I think you need the experience of college, detached from family and independent."

She is outspoken about her pursuit of a husband—to be acquired by the noncollege girl by twenty, by the college girl in her early twenties. By that time she feels that she will know what she is looking for in a husband. "You're still growing. You get married when you're eighteen and you meet another man you like." She expects to defer to her husband's career. "The husband has to have the more important career. I don't want to get my heart set. My career might conflict with his. I would like to work, though, for a few years. My husband (as yet unselected) might go on for a doctorate."

She wants to work for a year or two after marriage and in the somewhat distant future, perhaps after the children go to school, though such work seems unconnected with a career.

The idea of "fun" pervades the peer-oriented girl's thinking about marriage and work. She wants a life more exciting than her mother's and she sees this as outside the home. "I don't want to be just a housewife. You can clean up just so many times. I probably wouldn't have anything to do during the day." "I want to get out in the world. I might put children in a nursery or get somebody to keep them." "I don't know what I want to be. I'm not that ambitious. But I wouldn't want to waste my education just being a wife. Maybe I'll be a teacher. Teachers are needed and I can be finished by the time my children come home."

She would like the fun of adolescence to pervade the future, and she indicates that children may interfere. When will children interfere least with her fun? she asks herself. "It's good to have children when you're young, so you can party afterwards." Or, "I don't want kids right away, I want to have fun first." "If you get married immediately, you might have children." "I want to see the world first instead of staying in New York all my life having kids."

The lower-class girl who is fun-oriented during adolescence often feels that her fun ends here. Marriage is a grim affair. "You can never know what happens. No money is left after the bills are paid." "Sometimes I think I should let him work. My husband should be able to support me." [9]

The peer-oriented girl may acknowledge that her "fun" is too rigidly circumscribed, that she goes around too much with the same crowd and likes everything everybody else likes. She sometimes expresses distaste for the rule of her peers and feels that after high school subjugation to peers is not necessary. She seems to be leaving the door open for more autonomous considerations.

[9] Konopka makes the very important point that the lower-class woman has a long tradition of working at exploitative jobs outside the home. Marriage could be an escape from such inevitabilities, but the lower-class girl isn't very optimistic (Gisela Konopka, *The Adolescent Girl in Conflict* [Englewood Cliffs, N.J.: Prentice-Hall, Inc., 1966], pp. 73-74).

five

THE
ADULT-ORIENTED
GIRL

The adult-oriented girl is the conservative carrier of
her parents' values. She identifies herself completely with her parents' generation and thereby abjures even a new variety of conformism that the generation of her peers might proffer. Her byword is "mama and papa know best."

HER CONFIRMATION BY PARENTS

Too much relation with mother

In contrast to the mother of the peer-oriented girl, the
adult-oriented girl's mother serves as the confidante for her daughter. "I can be completely honest with my mother. She won't get mad at me." "We've always talked." "I have heart-to-heart talks with her all the time. She's very understanding." "I tell her everything. We talk more like friends. She realizes what she thought and did when she was my age." "My mother knows, I don't have to confide. She knows practically everything I'm thinking."

The mother exercises strong control over her daughter. The daughter may chafe somewhat under the restrictions but she is basically accepting and grateful for such control. In this respect she differs conspicuously from the peer-oriented girl.

I depend a lot on her. In my whole being, I would want to follow her judgment.

My mother watches over us very closely. The first thing I thought, "She doesn't trust you." But now I feel I'd do the same thing. We get along good together. I don't want to do the things the others are doing. Friday and Saturday we play records and talk. What is there to disagree about? I respect my mother. Some parents are so soft on their kids and the kids treat them as if they were one of us, they "sass" them. It's usually to the mother.

You usually think the way your parents think but nobody wants to follow exactly what their parents do.

We [the children] are not treated as persons, we have nothing to say. But I usually find myself thinking the way my mother does.

Mothers are justified in their fears. They don't want their daughters to go out with somebody who will get them in an accident. They want the best for their daughters.

Growing up faster makes the rules unbearable. But most girls feel parents are what they should be.

I know my mother has lots of wisdom I can take heed of. I think I listen to her too much, especially when I hear the other girls talking. She is older and knows a lot.

Even the complaints of the adult-oriented girl are mild compared with those of other girls. "My mother's control is mostly rational but you don't realize it at the time. You want your independence." "Sometimes she asks me questions over and over. For instance, 'What time did you get home after baby sitting?' " "Once in a while she tries too much. When she sees she's doing it, she'll stop."

The adult-oriented girl is concerned more with the necessity for controls than with the desire for freedom. She wonders if she doesn't have too much freedom in the "juvenile" things (e.g., freedom with a car.)

The characteristic of stability that the daughter finds "ideal" in her mother is very different from the ideal in "externals" such as dress and manners specified by the peer-conformist. "Some girls may want to do more than their mothers but in the same line. . . ." "My mother had ambition—she wanted to do more than she did.

I feel she would if she could have." "I hope I can bring up my children as she did." "My mother is the stable factor in the family."

Too little relation with father

The adult-oriented girl rarely confides in her father, lamenting that he doesn't understand her or is too little concerned with her affairs. "He's not here or there." "He's a funny man who doesn't say much about anything. He treats me more like an adult. He'll ask my advice about relations with my mother or about gifts. 'Your mother doesn't understand,' he tells me." "I consult my father. I feel he should make some of the decisions too," one girl condescendingly admits.

His work or other interests are important to him, he doesn't have time for us, some girls say. "My father is very involved in his work. He gets very aggravated." "He loves his work. It is his life. I guess I worry about him. I can't see any individual keeping up his pace." "He doesn't care too much. With six children, there are so many problems. It doesn't seem to bother him. Most of the responsibility is with my mother."

An occasional adult-oriented girl expresses fondness for her father. "I don't talk with him about my social life as with my mother. I talk with him about books, music, his job, or college. Most girls aren't terribly close to their fathers even though they are fond of them."

She indicates that she is respectful of the responsibilities that her father assumes. Such feelings aren't usually articulated by the peer-conformist. "I respect him." "Any time I need my father, he will be there. His sense of responsibility is overwhelming." "He would do anything for his family, even dig ditches. He turns his pay over to my mother. She gives him what he needs." "His prime virtue is integrity."

From the picture she paints of her involvement with her mother and her acceptance of parental controls at a time when girls generally turn from family to peers, we may infer that the adult-oriented girl has been confirmed as the good one (if she obeys) from her earliest years so that even now she affirms herself as the good girl who obeys her parents and other authority.

LITTLE INVESTMENT IN AUTONOMY

The adult-oriented girl's goals and vision are provided by adults. They are the yardstick by which she measures the rightness of her actions. "I am made by my family and my class," is her byword. "Children develop the interests their parents have," she concludes fatalistically. She has little sense of herself as autonomous, apart from her family. Any rebellion on her part is weak and futile.

Sometimes she emphasizes the female-linked impediments to autonomy, the passivity and submissiveness of girls, so that we may assume that she came from a family where the girl was expected to be good but the boy not necessarily so. "Girls are generally conformists. They have less tendency to stand up for ideas of their own. They agree rather than cause an issue. This isn't true of boys. Boys argue more." "Girls are very mixed up intellectually and politically. There are so many opinions going around about everything."

Her assessment of her body, of how far to go sexually, of who among her peers is "in" and who is "out" is determined primarily by her parents' dicta. Her appraisal of political issues follows the lines set down by parents and her appraisal of historic or literary issues follows the dictates of teachers. Her thought and action are circumscribed by what the "authorities" think or say. Some of her values, such as the importance of friendliness and popularity, may be similar to the peer-oriented girl's but derive from an adult source. Parents as well as peers may demand that a girl be friendly and seek peer approval.[1]

The adult-oriented girl's self-image of passivity seems to bear out the Freudian conception of the passive nature of woman. Woman

---

[1] "If peer expectations seem to stress peer approval to the detriment of achievement, parent expectations seem to stress both," according to Mathilda White Riley, John W. Riley, Jr., and Mary E. Moore, "Adolescent Values and the Riesman Typology: an Empirical Analysis," in Seymour Martin Lipset and Leo Lowenthal (eds.), *Culture and Social Character: The Work of David Riesman Reviewed* (New York: The Free Press, 1961), p. 378.

sees herself as biologically inferior to man, according to the Freudian theory of psychology which was conceived and embellished within the purview of a patriarchal society.[2]

In her two-volume work on *The Psychology of Women*, Helene Deutsch expands Freud's thesis on the little girl's turn from activity to passivity and posits as a basic axiom the masochistic nature of woman, her elemental need to be submissive, passive, and dependent.[3] The adult-oriented girl generally portrays this picture.

BEING PRUDENT VERSUS HAVING FUN

The adult-oriented girl considers prudence a cardinal virtue. She is not likely to do things "just for the fun of doing them" when such activity "is the exact opposite of what we know

[2] According to Freud, the little girl early senses her inferiority when she discovers that, unlike the little boys around her, she has no penis; this is a profound and shocking experience. She turns away from her first love, her mother, who is also an inferior being. A more passive little girl as a result of this degrading experience, she turns covetous eyes toward her father, who might hopefully give her a male child to compensate for her lack of a penis. Sigmund Freud, "Female Sexuality" (1931), in *Collected Papers*, V (London: The Hogarth Press, 1950), 259-272; *An Outline of Psychoanalysis* (New York: W. W. Norton & Company, Inc., 1949), pp. 97-99. (First published in German, 1940.) The passive adult-oriented girl described in my study does not turn away from her mother nor does she turn covetous eyes toward her father.

Penis envy has become a byword in describing the plight of woman, but some objections have been raised to this male-oriented theory even among Freudians themselves. Ernest Jones, Freud's definitive biographer, notes, "There is a healthy suspicion growing that men analysts have been led to adopt an unduly phallo-centric view. . . , the importance of the female organs being correspondingly underestimated. Women have on their side contributed to the general mystification by their secretive attitude towards their own genitals and by displaying a hardly disguised preference for interest in the male organ." ("The Early Development of Female Sexuality," in *Papers on Psycho-analysis* [5th ed.; Baltimore: The Williams & Wilkins Co., 1949], p. 438; read at the Tenth International Congress of Psycho-analysis, 1927). Anatomical structure promotes this preference for the male organ, says Phyllis Greenacre: "The man's organs are central and visible, whereas the woman's are mysteriously secreted" (*Trauma, Growth and Personality* [New York: W. W. Norton & Company, Inc., 1952], p. 257).

[3] Helene Deutsch, *The Psychology of Women* (New York: Grune & Stratton, Inc., 1944).

is the accepted standard of behavior." About Holden Caulfield in *The Catcher in the Rye,* she says, "It's stupid, pushing people out of windows, raising hell in subways. It is done without any thought of the consequences." She feels that teen-agers are not so emotional or so confused, though they may sometimes pretend to be. Moreover, "Nobody swears like that," she says, though she concedes that Salinger often captures the language of the teen-ager.

Her prudence is further demonstrated in her discussion of *Lord of the Flies.* "It's interesting to find out the psychology that comes about while kids are alone, without adult supervision and control," she maintains. "Kids were looking for something unusual, outside of their normal lives. The boys revert back to savages, even to the point of killing their fellows. They're brought back to reality by the arrival of a ship and its adult members. Kids would like to be free of parental controls, but this is what would happen. They don't want to hear this."

Adolescence is, ideally, a time of experimentation, whether in sex play, in banter with boys and with other girls, or in artistic or intellectual creation. In experimenting, the girl takes risks, she "lets herself go." The overemphasis on prudence as a way of life places an enormous impediment on the adult-oriented girl's freedom to experiment.

The adult-oriented girl reveals her orientation in her criticism of the Beatniks. What are their goals, what is their purpose in life, she wants to know. Are they self-disciplined?

They don't have too much goal in life. They want to sit around and loaf.

At parties they like to get drunk and have their kicks. They talk about sexual affairs.

They don't care what they do as long as it's pleasurable. They're looking for kicks.

They believe only they and not others [the teachers] are right. They're fresh, trouble-makers.

They conform to their own patterns of dress and behavior. They consider themselves people with a purpose, a message, but they don't give anything. It's an excuse for being lazy and shiftless.

They're sloppy, have no pride in themselves.

More sympathetically,

They shouldn't be so much criticized. I don't agree with all of them but they have a lot to offer, for example, in the way of music.

HER AFFIRMATION OF PARENTAL
VALUES AND EXPECTATIONS

The parents of the adult-oriented girl expect that she
will be socially mobile, if she is lower class, and that she will retain her class position, if she is higher class. These social gymnastics cannot be managed on her own, as the peer-oriented girl claims, but only with the aid of parents. Her adherence to parental values and her needing parental assistance to achieve these values often mean alienation from groups of peers.

The lower-class girl indicates some of the difficulties that ensue in her attempt to rise in class—

Says a lower-class girl:

When the parents are educated and have money, their daughter can't be an ordinary girl. The kids are brought up to go to school. The parents clamp down. If I lived there [in a middle-income cooperative], I'd have the opportunity to meet friends on that level. Our parents are all out of the same boat. We're common people. My mother and father try to raise us so that we'll meet better people, not stay in our home.

Says a lower-middle-class girl:

Children develop the interests their parents have—the theaters, the parties, the books. A lot of the girls in my high school class come from high-income families and have more money to spend on books and on education. The girls expect a lot from you in cultural things. They expect you to be able to go with them to the theater or on bus trips. They don't understand.

An upper-middle-class girl repeats that what a girl is, is determined by her parents, and one of the results, for her, is alienation from peers of lower classes. In her disqualification of lower-class peers as possible companions, she refers to the defects not only of peers but also of their parents.

Out of school I tend to be snobbish when I really don't want to be, to girls whose parents are uneducated. I don't even like to admit this. I have practically nothing in common with them. They don't care about education. My crowd is interested in literature, art, and music.

The goals of the adult-oriented girl are as nonrestrictive (or as restrictive) as those of her adult models. In the sample, intellectual goals are at least as important as popularity among peers. Whether an adult-oriented girl is pretty and popular or quiet and studious, she is generally more engrossed in being "intellectual" than in being "popular." "As you grow older, boys are not such a preoccupation as in fifth or sixth grade when you first discover the opposite sex. Then you haven't developed cultural interests yet. Maybe then, you want it just for attention." "Most of the time I sit home and read. Nothing is more important to me than education." "Now I'm going steady but it wouldn't bother me if I wasn't."

The adult-oriented girl generally expresses an interest in broadening her intellectual and aesthetic horizons. Such pursuits are a means of maintaining an upper-class position. "Most girls don't know much about music and art," an upper-middle-class girl condescendingly points out. "They were never exposed to it. 'We all can't go to the opera like your parents,' they say to me."

Such pursuits are a means of expanding horizons for the lower-class (or working-class) girl. They open for her a new world. "I read mostly teen-age things: *Seventeenth Summer* by Maureen Daly and *Fifteen* by Beverly Hale. They show what a girl would go through," says one slum resident and adds hopefully, "I'm trying to go into classics." "I carry the dictionary with me," another girl from a lower-class family admits, and her sister adds, "I read the books on the reading lists that the teachers give." An attractive and knowledgeable working-class girl is learning art and music from her middle-class friends. She studies paintings with them and they go together to plays and concerts. "My mother wants me to better myself," she explains. The mobile lower-class girl is sometimes very disdainful of her "rotten apple" siblings who aren't interested even in graduating from high school.

Education is the basis of all living, a lower-middle-class girl from the suburbs suggests. "When man is pushed back into nature (as

was true in *The Lord of the Flies*), he can't adjust to it. It makes
you realize you can't just have a little education, you have to have
a lot in order to get along."

The lower-class adult-oriented girl, while still strongly dependent on adults, has gone farther toward autonomy than her upper-
class counterpart. The goal for the lower-class girl is change, while
the aims of the upper-class girl are conservative and her goal is
stability.

CONCERN WITH HER BODY

Associated with the adult-oriented girl's self-image of
passivity is an image of "modesty." "Girls basically have a nature
of modesty," says one girl. "They were created for reproduction. It
is more in their nature to be modest." Her own "shy and modest
nature" and her parents' dicta are the determining factors in her
reluctance to take a shower in gym class. "All girls in gym class are
shy about dressing," she maintains. "They won't take showers with
other girls. It's true almost universally." "We get notes from our
parents saying we can't take showers. It's planted in us. I don't think
we're ashamed of our body." "I wouldn't ordinarily disrobe at home.
I'd feel uncomfortable even with my mother." "I guess it's just a
natural thing that your parents have taught you to keep yourself to
yourself."

"Modest" and self-effacing, she derives her sense of worth as a
woman from a man's approval and not from pleasure and pride in
what she has to give. This "modesty" and shyness reflect little confidence in her own sexuality and indicate little expectation of sensation and pleasure from her own body.

The adult-oriented girl, like other girls, is concerned about her
face, hair, and figure. For her, too, menstruation brings to the fore
any ambivalence she has about her body. But in addition she seems
to approach menstruation with greater trepidation. While, for example, the peer-oriented girl seems to wait anxiously for her first
period as an indication of her eligibility to join the ranks of womanhood, the adult-oriented girl seems to fear growing up. She remembers being frightened the first time she menstruated. "I was very
upset at first. I didn't want to have the responsibility."

HER RELATIONS WITH BOYS

Adult-oriented girls of all ages vary considerably in
their relations with boys. Some don't date at all or don't date very
often while others date frequently.

Going steady is a threat to some girls' emotional security, and
that is enough to rule it out. The "fun" aspect is not mentioned
when the adult-oriented girl indicates her lack of desire to go steady,
as it is with the peer-oriented girl. "Before I went steady but I'm
cooling it," one lower-class adult-oriented girl explains. "I realized
that something I had done was not good for me. At first it's so rosy,
but then come the problems. My friend went steady, she got pregnant, quickly got married, and now they're ready to split up. My
boy friends are just friends and my mother knows who they are
and their parents."

Other adult-oriented girls do want to go steady, with marriage
in view. They are not willing to endure the risks, uncertainties, and
rebuffs that come with postponing the choice of a mate. "Some girls
are looking for future husbands—very decent girls, more my standard." The serious girl may start even in high school to "push" her
erstwhile suitor into an educational and occupational program that
will underwrite what she wants in a husband. "I want him to combine his job with a community college so he can become a teacher,"
announces one lower-middle-class girl. Another quiet, studious lower-
middle-class girl who writes a letter to her boy friend every night
maintains that "knowing someone cares about you gives you a very
good security feeling."

The adult-oriented girl, more than other girls, expresses caution
about "going too far" in sexual relations, although "going too far"
has a variety of meanings. To one girl, the "middle group" tends
to kissing while petting is prevalent only among the "wild girls."
To another girl, "petting is commonplace. Most girls, though, are
pretty good—no intercourse."

It is not her peers but her parents whom she fears. "You have
fear of your parent's voice. There's a fear instilled in you it's wrong.
A person should have respect for her parents and her family." "Your
mother tells you what's right and wrong." Having been forewarned

about the dire consequences of sexual indulgence, she fears self-recrimination: "You know it's wrong." Sometimes she says that she fears God.

"IN" WITH THE GROUP?

The adult-oriented girl does not seem on her way toward greater positive relationship with others in a world larger than her own family or desired class.

When she is an upper-class girl of the "proper" race and religion, where so many status and security rewards are provided at home— the private school, the country club, the inheritance, the family name—she has little incentive to leave her nurturing environs or to wage battle that others might be admitted to her privileged status.

If she sees herself stigmatized by class, religion, or race, she is likely to acquiesce in this stigmatization rather than to fight against it. A lower-class girl may try to change her status but she rarely envisions any basic change in the social structure that permits such stigmatization.

There seems little significant difference between adult- and peer-oriented girls in the stereotyped perception of racial and ethnic out-groups.

Among the adult-oriented girls, for instance, the girl who is not Negro often deprecates Negroes. "The Negro girls gang up. A lot of time they want to make issues to show they're mistreated," asserts a lower-middle-class girl. "Negroes sometimes don't help you in respecting them. They act in a rude manner, they're cocky, defensive, sort of wild and showy. It's been instilled in them since the Civil War," explains an upper-middle-class girl. The attitude of quiet indignation expressed by the two non-Negro girls quoted above seems at variance with their studious, adult-oriented manner. Both are highly sensitive to their own somewhat precarious marginality —for one, her lower-middle-class membership in a higher-class peer group, for the other, her Chinese background. It may be supposed that they are attempting to put their own self-doubts to rest by scapegoating the Negro.

The Puerto Rican or Negro girl often deprecates herself. "The

Puerto Ricans worry about having a good time, they don't think about tomorrow," asserts a lower-class Puerto Rican girl. "Most Negroes are ignorant. They think that overnight they should become what the white man is today," maintains a lower-middle-class Negro girl.

The Negro girl who aspires to college and career or who is surrounded in everyday living by a dominant white majority expresses acute sensitivity about discrimination and prejudice. "I got 84 and I'm off honor society but a white girl who failed math, they kept her in the honor society." "White girls have more chance to be a cheerleader." She may try to compensate for her color degradation through personal excellence in sports or music or dance, in which she knows that a Negro is permitted to excel. "I go out for sports. Negro girls have more vitality. Negroes can excel there. I hold my head high." She perpetually reminds herself that she dresses better or looks better or is more talented than white girls.

The Jewish girl sees herself stereotyped as the girl with nice clothes who is smart and thinks she is superior. Disparaging remarks —"Jew Hill," "cheap, dirty Jew," "smart Jew," "damn Jew"—are occasionally made by her peers but never in her presence, she says. "You'd never hear, 'You damn Protestant,'" she complains.

POLITICAL COMMITMENT

As with the high school girl generally, the adult-oriented girl indicates little interest in politics or political issues. She usually claims membership in the political party of her parents and accepts their judgment. "My mother belongs to the Democratic club. I guess we're Democratic." "It's pretty far removed." If she were older, she conjectures, maybe she would show more interest. "I think it's more in college." "Maybe when I'm twenty-one, I'll look into things and see what's happening." Her interest might be greater, she thinks, if she were a boy. "Girls aren't interested in politics as much as boys." "Many boys want to go into some phase of public life."

When the adult-oriented girl is asked specific questions about the

Peace Corps, a humanitarian note creeps in much more frequently than with the peer-oriented girl. She gives as her reasons for interest in the Peace Corps: "The idea of helping people appeals to me." "It would be a work experience and I'd see a life altogether different from my own." "It would help me to understand them." Not all adult-oriented girls, though, would care for its hardships. "I can't bring myself to care about people who are millions of miles away," one girl confesses.

RELIGIOUS INVOLVEMENT

The adult-oriented girl is a regular church-goer. She usually goes with her family. One girl who doesn't go to church explains, "It has to start in your home, else it's difficult to feel strongly about it."

Religious organization is very important to her. She likes the sociability of church. "The youth groups have many activities. You go on hikes and hay rides and camping with kids who feel the way you do about your religion. You have Christian companionship."

Even more than the sociability, church membership and attendance provide a sense of continuity in her life. "I go to church Sunday and to Young People's Choir Thursday night. My two sisters go too. Ever since I remember I was in a church." "I wouldn't feel right if I didn't go to church." Church membership provides a sense of identity. "Out here I was the only Jew in my class. Then we found our identity—a Reform temple. We enjoyed it and became active." "Maybe I have an identity with all these people. The songs, the chants—I like to sing them."

The adult-oriented girl appears to be searching for a strong, father figure. She seems to want continual confirmation of her goodness from a strong parental figure. She sees God as the Creator, the Prime Mover, who makes the world comprehensible. "He started civilization; there would be nothing without Him."

Her God is a moralistic God who influences behavior. "He helps us know right from wrong." "I put myself in what He would do. That's what I try to do." "He's always watching you. If you couldn't do something in front of him, you shouldn't do it at all." "Everybody fears God. They know what He will do if they do those bad things."

Her God intercedes in her behalf. He will take care of things, but only if she meets him half way. "I pray for God to keep us alive and safe." "Times when I'm in trouble or school work isn't going well, I turn to Him." "I pray for the family." "I ask for help but I know it's really me. I have free will though He's in back of me in a way." "I pray to God but not for tests. According to the Bible, God helps those who help themselves." "Even if the prayers are unanswered, you have to believe in it first and keep praying. If the favor is not granted, maybe He thinks that what you are asking is not good for you."

An adult-oriented girl whose father has died finds solace in the reckoning of the afterlife. "God caused my father to die. There is a life after death, otherwise his death makes no sense. If he led a good life, it will earn his entrance into heaven."

The conceptualization of the adult-oriented girl may be likened to Freud's explanation of the function of religion as a re-creation of the child's dependent relation to his father.[4] At puberty, the girl displaces the feelings of adoration of and dependence on the father onto the idea of God.[5]

MARRIAGE OR CAREER

In her talk about plans for higher education, marriage, and possible career, there seems little difference between the peer-oriented and the adult-oriented girl. More than those in generations that preceded her, she is likely to be oriented toward further study after high school. She generally looks forward to marriage by twenty if she does not plan to study beyond high school; otherwise, in her early twenties.

The vision of education as enriching family life is rare for either the peer- or adult-oriented girl. Though marriage is definitely in the

---

[4] Sigmund Freud, *The Future of an Illusion* (New York: Doubleday & Company, Inc., 1957; first published, 1927).

[5] Ernest Jones, "Some Problems of Adolescence," in *Papers on Psycho-analysis* (5th ed.; Baltimore: The Williams & Wilkens Co., 1949), p. 403. Delivered originally in 1922.

cards within a few years, it is thought about as an end-state, a termination point, rather than a beginning. One atypical statement comes from an upper-middle-class adult-oriented girl who speaks of using her education in the service of her family. With education, she says, "You can enjoy life better, expose your kids to more things, you can read books and understand them better. When you don't have kids any more, you can work and really have something to do."

The girl wants to work for a year or two after marriage and in the somewhat distant future, perhaps after the children go to school, but such work entails no real involvement in a career.[6] She engages in little serious speculation about career choices, though she mentions the possibility of the customary service fields appropriated by women: secretary, nurse, or teacher. "Career and marriage somehow don't mix," is a common response. "The husband has to have the more important career. I don't want to get my heart set. My career might conflict with his." "Boys have to earn a living. They're more stable than girls, more interested in their education." The "career" is a job to go back to "if the marriage doesn't work out or something like that," or "if something happens to your husband."[7]

The rare girl for whom career is more important than marriage says she probably won't marry. "I don't want to get married," affirms one lower-class career-oriented girl. "I think marriage interferes with your career. Once a girl gets married, she just stays home." So too the upper-middle-class careerist who wants to make a name for herself through her writing asserts, "I don't want family and children

[6] She will probably be getting married younger than her mother and having her children earlier. Though almost a third of the country's married women are employed outside the home, at least half the women workers are over forty, and this is a distant perspective for the adolescent girl.

[7] The point is increasingly being made that it is not primarily the husband or the lack of opportunities that limit the wife's occupational attainments but rather the wife herself, with her image of the "feminine" woman performing the nurturant expressive functions, leaving the instrumental functions to men. This country has no tradition of the upper-class woman devoting herself to intellectual or artistic attainment. *See* Alice S. Rossi, "Equality Between the Sexes: An Immodest Proposal," *Daedalus* (Spring 1964), pp. 607-652; Ellen and Kenneth Keniston, "An American Anachronism: The Image of Women and Work," *The American Scholar*, XXXIII, No. 3 (Summer 1964), 355-375; Betty Friedan, *The Feminine Mystique* (New York: W. W. Norton & Company, Inc., 1963).

to stand in the way of my career. I want a completely self-disciplined career."

The adult-oriented girl is the mirror-image of what her mother would like her to be. She may be accumulating knowledge and good grades and participating in school and community activities. She may have competence in receiving but not in producing ideas. She is often a highly moralistic girl with a tinge of self-righteousness, carrying on the battle of her elders against more deviant peers. She is embedded in her family, her class, her religion, and her race and is not yet free to move out on her own. She is not an autonomous person who makes choices and takes responsibility. Her choices are made by others. "They" are responsible. And so it will probably be with her husband. She will continue to affirm herself as the "good" one who does her husband's bidding, and presumably she will select a husband who will confirm her in this fashion.

six

THE DELINQUENT:
HER SEARCH
FOR RELATION

WHO IS THE DELINQUENT GIRL?

Delinquency is a legal category. A girl is declared delinquent by a court for such deviant behavior as sexual promiscuity or else truancy, running away, serious physical aggression, or theft. She is usually brought to court by her mother or the police or referred by the school or a social agency. Following an adjudication of delinquency, she may be placed on probation or sent to a delinquency institution or a mental hospital. The girl committing such deviant acts is more likely to be brought to court and institutionalized if she is lower class.

Most delinquency among girls involves sexual deviancy. The delinquent girl bears the stigma of having been declared "bad" by family, peers, and society. The outstanding features of her life history and present circumstances are:

1. "Abandonment" by her family—physical or emotional
2. Her "bad" behavior in reaction to this abandonment
3. The "badness" leading her inevitably to seek other "bad" adolescents as accepting companions
4. The final crystallization of her bad personification in her relationships with other "bad" peers.

The features of this delinquent pattern were found both among the girls inside the hospital and among those in the community.

ABANDONMENT AT HOME—PHYSICAL
AND EMOTIONAL

The delinquent girl comes from a barren home where
since early childhood there was no enduring warm personal relationship. She may have been physically abandoned or, more likely,
she was neglected and rejected. In any case, neither her parents nor
any parental substitute was "there" to give either direction and
guidance or sympathy and love when it was needed.

The mother seemed preoccupied with her own living. The father, when he was present, was also detached and distant from his
daughter. He may have been embarrassed at any display of affection
or intimacy with her. He may fit the characterization given by his
daughter of a brutal or difficult man who fought with the grandparents or tried to rape her, his daughter, or was chased out of the
home by her mother because he wanted more children or didn't
support the ones he had.

Physical abandonment

In the extreme, the girl was physically abandoned by
her parents and spent much of her life with relatives or in foster
homes or institutions. When substitute parents took over, the relationship always seemed transitory. Parents, and adults in general,
are emotionally distant.

Though the mother of this abandoned girl is an ephemeral figure who darted in and out between men or was weighed down with
other problems, and though the girl was raised by others, her mother,
nevertheless, is the symbol of her roots, her source of identification
and belongingness. The girl holds on for dear life to thoughts of
this mother though she knows she is holding on to a mirage. The
anxiety connected with abandonment is evident when the girl sees
her mother or when she anticipates seeing her but the mother doesn't
visit her and doesn't write.

An attractive Puerto Rican girl expresses the ambivalence dra-
matically. "My mother used to beat me; she once tried to kill me,"
and she shows the scar where her mother ragefully cut her with a
knife when her father followed her to an apartment where her

mother was living with another man. "But even though she did these things, I want to see her. She ran away and we never found her." There seems to be a concatenation of feelings. "She is not an ideal mother but she is *mine*. Having a mother makes me like other girls. Did I drive her away? If she won't love me, who will?" Frustration and guilt may lead to aggression, and the girl's effort to remake her mother into an idealized model may give way to the desire to retaliate.

Over and over, delinquent girls at the hospital tell tales of abandonment by their mothers. Felicia, Puerto Rican, explains that she has been at the hospital for eight months and hasn't seen her family for four. "I've lived out ever since I was a baby," she says. "In the City Hospital and Youth House and Children's Center and St. Agnes and St. Anne—no, not St. Anne—and Children's Foundling Home, and in foster homes—mostly in foster homes." Her mother is going to have a baby by her current boy friend. "She had one last year, didn't she?" I ask. "She can have another one this year," Felicia says gravely.

Zelda, a tiny Negro girl, explains that her grandmother died when she was six and gave her to an aunt. She has her aunt's phone number "in case of an emergency." In her ten months at the hospital she has had no visitors. Zelda's mother does appear one weekend. Zelda rushes to embrace her but her mother stand-offishly greets her with, "What happened to your shoes and your dress, Zelda?"

Frances, an untidy baby-faced blonde, reminisces, as she eats ice cream, that at home they never had desserts except on special holidays like Christmas and Thanksgiving. Her mother is coming to see her before her birthday. She will probably give her two dollars and maybe a crinoline. . . . But days pass and Frances gets no mail from her mother. She becomes increasingly frustrated. It's only her foster mother anyway, she declares, but she could send a card at least.

The search for male attachment is often made to replace an absent parental attachment. In the tales that are told of love and woe, a recurring fear of abandonment is expressed. This is illustrated by fifteen-year-old Carmen, a Puerto Rican girl, who has a rapid succession of superficial relationships with boys. The second of seven children, Carmen has lived most of her years with her strict paternal grandparents except for brief interludes with her parents, who lived nearby. She has a history of truanting and finally of running away and being reported to the police. She was sent to a Catholic juvenile delinquency institution and then to a mental hospital.

Carmen writes the name of her boy friend, Angelo, over her clothes and on her school papers. But she decides to "quit" Angelo and substitute loftier goals. Girls should only kiss boys on the cheek, no hugging or necking, she insists. She's a virgin and isn't interested in boys. She wants to go home and study, go to night school and make something of herself. She would like to be a social worker and help people or a nurse or a foreign reporter who travels over the world and writes for the front pages. She once wanted to be a nun. She interrupts her ruminations when she sees David outside and calls boisterously to him.

Carmen shows a preoccupation with sexual intercourse and child-bearing when a friend reads a letter from a small-town aunt. "They fuck too much there," Carmen insists. "The people in Honolulu, Hawaii fuck too much, too. They have too many children, children every day."

A few weeks later Carmen introduces a new boy friend, Raymond, and wears his hat. But after two days she is worried about Raymond. Did he quit her? Should she quit him first and thus salvage some injured esteem? Some of the girls tell her he now goes with Anita. No, she won't quit Raymond yet, she must find out what's happening. She prints in large letters on her notebook, "Mr. and Mrs. Raymond Gonzales."

In addition to worries about boys, Carmen is concerned about her mother. Her father hit her mother again and her mother left home and returned to her lover. She fears abandonment not only by her boy friends but also by her mother. She seems to demand from her boy friend an attachment sufficiently strong to make up for the absence of one with her fleeting, unstable mother.

Emotional abandonment

The delinquent girl's abandonment by her family is sometimes not physical but emotional. The girl has been so neglected or disregarded that she feels abandoned.

She may be a lower-class girl who lives in a world where an immature mother scurries from one man to another, neglecting her children, the fruits of a previous passion; where a succession of "bad" and anonymous men join the "family" for a time and then leave; where, between man and woman and woman and daughter, warfare and truce unceasingly alternate. Her mother's sexual encounters with various men are in full view in her over-crowded tenement; even momentary privacy is at a premium.

She may be a middle-class girl whose mother does not want the responsibility of this child. The mother is more involved with men or coiffures or other siblings than with her daughter.

HER "BAD" BEHAVIOR AND THE SEARCH FOR "BAD" COMPANIONS

The girl who has been abandoned by her family is lonely and depressed.[1] She responds to the abandonment with frantic "bad" behavior calculated to force her parents' attention. At an early age she has temper tantrums. Much later she truants from school or runs away from home overnight and possibly has her first sexual encounter.

The family or other authority reacts to her behavior by calling her "bad," and after such repeated confirmations she comes to see herself as "bad." She has now suffered a double injury: the "bad" personification is added to her loneliness and depression. She is beginning to feel like an outsider with her peers, who by their glances or their talk indicate that she is "no good" and no longer belongs. She must seek a new group of accepting peers and since she is "bad," she expects to find companionship only with other "bad" persons. Those who will accept her are likely to be in the same boat. She is compelled now to live out her badness, to make it a reality, since this is consistent with the person she has become.

---

[1] Gisela Konopka speaks about the distinctive plight of the delinquent girl as loneliness accompanied by despair, loneliness which sees no way out. She "yearns for friendship but seems to have little capacity for it."

Konopka describes the "wearying and insidious cycle: . . . the girl feels abandoned—frequently she really is abandoned—searches for friendship, becomes abandoned again, or abandons others, because she cannot hold on to people, is being disappointed and disappoints others" (*The Adolescent Girl in Conflict* [Englewood Cliffs, N.J.: Prentice-Hall, Inc., 1966], pp. 40, 41, 103).

She hears further name-calling and so the vicious cycle proceeds.

Her pursuit of men is often frantic and propulsive. She is unable to control the pace. "Let's see, how many guys have I been going with," asks the popular Sally and begins to enumerate them. She has never gone with any boy more than two weeks. With Joe it is now three. She plans to marry Joe until she hears that a good-looking boy has just arrived. "If I can go with him, I'll quit Joe," she says. Ethel, enamored of Ralph, likes Tony too, who is in her class and has such blue eyes. "It's very funny," she muses. "I say, 'I love you, I love you, I love you' to a boy and then suddenly I don't like him any more and I like somebody else. Something must be wrong with me."

Relationships with boys may be less frantic and more opportunistic but with no more continuity or fidelity. Sara, age fourteen, recounts her problem: A boy of twenty-two who is coming to see her tomorrow has limited his companionship with girls exclusively to her. But she wants to go with the boy she met at the dance yesterday who is seventeen. She is afraid the boy of twenty-two will beat up the seventeen-year-old when he finds out. A few days later, Sara turns to the older boy. He came to see her on three successive days and gave her money, she says, in explaining her transfer of affection.

When she is with a boy, life is "wonderful." Otherwise, life is "terrible."

Yesterday Fay seemed apathetic, but today she is gleeful, almost hysterical. Visitors are coming and she is expecting a friend. She sits on the floor, stretches out her legs, and asks Sally how she does it, with her legs up from the ground or down. Fay says she has been waiting so long, she hasn't done it for eight months. She removes her jeans and puts on a tight skirt. The tighter the better, she replies gleefully to a girl who comments on the tightness.

The delinquent cannot bide her time. She cannot endure present discomfort for future advantage. Too often there is no future advantage. She searches for a man who can provide some modicum of relation.

It seems that the lure of sexual excitement is not overpowering for the delinquent girl. She may express momentary ecstasy, but she also indicates that she "can take it or leave it."

Fay, the prototype of the delinquent, wears heavy make-up and her clothes are skin-tight. She recounts with glee her sexual experiences but shortly afterwards appears isolated and despondent. She explains that she became part of a "fast crowd," cut classes, and stayed out overnight. It was with this crowd that she had her first sexual experience. "After that I just had to have it," she feels. "But I've changed now. I don't need it any more." If born again, "I would be a nice, decent little girl. I wouldn't run away from home or have sex relations with boys."

Jean wonders why she should go out on dates, if the boys are only looking to see if the stories about her are true.

The delinquent girl is so overwhelmed by her need for relation that she can be neither autonomous nor loving. She cannot really play in the sexual encounter, she cannot gain pleasure from the sexual experience as an end in itself since sex serves always as the means to keep a boy or to display her power or prestige. Since she expects all relations to be fleeting, she is perpetually looking further.

There is much association of sex with rape and violence, either in real life or in fantasy as revealed in the stories on projective tests. The accounts, for instance, of an attractive Puerto Rican girl, shunted from father to mother to grandmother, are filled with sexual violence:

A woman strangles a man, is jailed for life.

She hates men, hates people.

A man rapes a woman, then he sees his mistake.

A man escapes from prison, rapes a lady, shoots himself.

The descriptions of hostile encounters with men are frequent—such accounts as Sally's who tells about the cold, snowy winter evening when she was walking to her corner wearing boots without shoes, her head down to escape the wind. A man accosts her and says, "Come into the hall with me or I'll tie your mouth."

The delinquent often describes men as "bad." Will I introduce her to some good boys? one girl implores. "Men are no good, they mess a girl's life up," says another. "They beat women and then they go away. A boy needs a father but a girl needs only a mother. Why don't you tell the girls not to go with boys," she pleads. "You know more about this and you should tell them what to do."

There is much association of the body with cleanliness and uncleanliness. When the delinquent girl is asked to complete the sentence, "My body is . . . ," she almost invariably adds, "clean." The sexually promiscuous delinquent who says: "My body it always does what I want it to," seems the exception. We may speculate: how much is this emphasis on cleanliness a general cultural phenomenon among women in our society and how much does the delinquent girl see her own body as unclean as a result of her sexual experiences and her "bad" personification?

THE SEXUALIZATION OF RELATIONSHIPS

The delinquent girl who was observed appears to sexualize most relationships. Her language, both in quantity and quality, is the language of body. Her interaction with others is just as likely to be physical as verbal, not only with men but also with women. She kisses and hugs and fist-fights other girls and lies down with her head in another girl's lap—all of this without any necessary homosexual overtones.

Her encounters with boys are usually spoken of in sexual terms. She describes the boys' insistence upon sexual relations. A boy kept hitting her in the breast at a dance so she hit him on the "prick." Another boy pulled her toward him and said, "Put it in, put it in." "What do you mean?" she asks him, and then she understands. If she is a gang girl, she tells about the pressure for sexual relations that the boy gang imposes upon her. The insistence, though, does not always come from the boy. The girls tell about Rose inching up to her partner as she dances with him. Finally he says, with apparent disdain, "Here it is, if you want it."

Her encounters with girls too are often sexualized. A girl may be seen lying on top of another. A girl kisses me and asks me to "go with" her. Another asks to "put [her] finger up [my] hole." Such sexualization seems a combination of bravado and an attempt to express intimacy with another female. Often indicated is a fear of genital involvement with a girl: a "lesbie," or "don't lesbie me," a girl jibes in derision. One boisterous girl illustrates her drive-stigma conflict. She writes on her arm with ink, "I love Mae." She carves "Mae" on her thigh with a pin. Several weeks later she bravely asserts, "I used to like girls but I don't any more."

The sexualization of relationships is revealed most primitively in a girl's preoccupation, often in the vernacular, with the sex life of almost everything that passes through her mind: a teen-ager on the cover of *Life* magazine, the mice, a dead grandmother, and the observer.

The teen-ager on the cover of *Life* is pointed to with disdain: "She prostitutes herself for money. It says so." (The article describes the dating habits of a "typical fourteen-year-old.") The animals on the ward are watched with rapt attention for any indication of sexual relations. A mouse is seen jumping on top of another. "They're fucking," a girl announces. "You'll get children that way," the mice are admonished.

Even memories of the dead grandmother are sexualized. A tiny Negro girl informs the group that when her grandmother died, she and her sister went to the morgue and pushed her grandmother's head into the coffin, then walked around and sat down. Soon they heard voices. The dead people got up and danced and her grandmother was heard to laugh and say something about "screwing" somebody. Only one girl expresses disbelief.

The description of her neighborhood has sexual overtones. Lois tells the girls what goes on in her neighborhood. White women with tight skirts and long orange and pearl earrings leaning against cars. They have dyed red hair and wear too much lipsick and mascara. And boys following you to the store. She had to get a cop's protection or else they would have done something to her.

From the first day on, the delinquent girl probes me about my sexual experiences. Her sequence of questions: "Do you have any children?" "Are you married?" "Are you a virgin?" And, "Did you have intercourse before you were old enough to know what it was all about?" "I know you are a virgin, you wouldn't be allowed to work here at the hospital unless you were," one girl says. "How would they know?" I ask. "It would be on your record," she replies.

How much this sexualization of relationships is a delinquent phenomenon and how much a lower-class phenomenon is not clear. Most, but not all, of the girls come from lower-class homes. All, of course, are in a sense captives of the group that may provide both the freedom and the incentive for such sex talk. I conjecture that, as with the bully-flunky interaction described below, the sexualization of relationships is both a lower-class and a delinquent phenomenon: one buttresses the other and, in addition, one is independent of the other.

EXPRESSION OF INCAPACITY: POWER AMONG PEERS

Another theme that pervades the delinquent girl's talk and her interaction with others is power. The delinquent girl seems to see life as a continual power struggle in which the strong impose their wills on the weak. Every bully has a scapegoat or a flunky. A girl constantly rates and rerates her peers and may alternately become the flunky or the bully, depending upon whether she gauges her peers as tougher and bolder or as weaker and more cowardly than herself.

The power motif permeates most roles in the two lower-class delinquent groups that were observed at the state hospitals. The sexually promiscuous girl is often power-oriented as is the boy-snatcher. But the prototype of this power-oriented world is the bully, who inundates her victim with physical and verbal abuse. "She pushes you around," the girls acknowledge. "She picks on people because she knows they can't fight, she fights dirty." The bully doesn't always work alone but has henchmen to support her. Ten to fifteen colored girls may "gang up" against a few Spanish girls or a girl whose father is colored and mother white or a girl who dresses better or has taken somebody's boy friend. On occasion, the bully and her henchmen may cut a victim's long and beautiful hair. If they can't beat with their hands, they may use knives.[2]

[2] It is interesting to note that of the 15 girls whom one group perceives as most likely to be "boss" or "bully," 12 (or 80 per cent) are either only children or

A girl may lack the assertiveness and the daring required to play the bully and instead becomes the passive, submissive follower or possibly the flunky or the scapegoat. The girl who allows herself to be the butt of the bully's jibes and jokes and threats (the scapegoat) or who acts with servility toward other girls, emptying their trays and washing their clothes (the flunky) is tormented in the demeaning fashion employed only by a blatantly power-oriented group. At play the girls throw the ball with obvious vengeance at her. When she ventures an innocent assertion, she is rebuked with, "Why are you such an instigator?" They laugh at her appearance and threaten to beat her up. They assign lowly duties to her and then verbally castigate her: "She doesn't keep clean. She doesn't want to wash her clothes. Her body is always smelling." One is reminded of the Indians' treatment, or former treatment, of the Untouchables: a segregation first by occupation, then by more personal attributes.

The least popular girl in the group is not the bully but the scapegoat or flunky.[3] Cowardice is the most deprecated quality among power-oriented girls and the scapegoat or flunky is a coward. She runs and cries but won't fight back unless her antagonist is smaller and weaker, at which time her own bully tendencies come forth. "I am the weakling," she seems to say to herself. "I can't pit my strength against the others either physically or verbally. Only my crying might save me." The scapegoat may combine her cowardice with "tattling" to staff and with occasional thefts which further provoke the group. The roles of flunky and scapegoat are debasing. The performer has no sense of "This is I," an active, assertive, independent being, but is tied as a slave to a master. (It is not only the flunky who does the bully's bidding. Any girl should carry her pride against the bully just so far, is the consensus: "I'd be crazy if I don't get her that book, and six girls with her!")

It appears that the staff who work closely with the delinquent girls either do not perceive the flunky role or do not recognize its

---

are the oldest among their siblings. Fifty-six per cent of the total group are only or oldest children. This difference is statistically significant at the .10 level.

[3] Of the six girls rated as least popular by their peers in the delinquent group, four were flunkies but none were bullies.

importance. On a four-point scale of dominance-submission: (1) bossy, a bully; (2) a leader, the girls like to follow her; (3) cooperative, helpful, goes along; and (4) a flunky, the staff at one of the state hospitals rate the two least popular girls in the group at (2.8), while the group rates them at (3.6).[4] The peer group and the staff also perceive these two least popular girls very differently on the dimension of self-restraint. On the scale: (1) ready to fight, has a temper; (2) usually OK, but sometimes can get very angry; (3) even-tempered, peaceful; and (4) gives up, won't fight back, the two least popular girls are rated (1.8) by the staff, (3.2) by the girls. The group sees these two flunkies more often as "giving up, won't fight back," the staff sees them as much more aggressive. Either the flunky is almost entirely a role among peers or else the staff glosses over or misperceives the servile activity of the flunky, associating her only with her more aggressive behavior.

The power-oriented girl desires mastery not only over other girls but also over property, though she is not so obsessed with the desire for property as is many a delinquent boy. Her actions imply, "What's yours is mine if I can get it and get away with it." Begging is acceptable behavior and is conspicuous during mealtime in one of the delinquent groups when the would-be bully who is not big enough or strong enough to play the bully role goes from one table to another begging food from timid, passive girls. The bully begs too, though she is discriminating in her choice of booty, beseeching the staff for jewelry, belts, and dresses, in contrast to her self-depreciating peer who begs for five cents or a cigarette.

The delinquent is peer-oriented. With no understanding or unharrassed adults to turn to, peer orientation is a necessity.[5] Friendships among peers, though, usually seem tenuous and are not based on any long-enduring involvements. Few genuine tears are shed

---

[4] Each girl checked her self-perception (HOW I AM), how she WOULD LIKE TO BE, and HOW EACH OF THE OTHER GIRLS IS on a four-point scale for various dimensions: for example, physical attractiveness, dominance-submission, sexuality-relations with boys, self-restraint, superiority-inferiority, and friendliness.

In addition, each girl rated every other girl on popularity—that is, whom she would like to be with in various activities.

[5] There were few gang girls in the groups I observed. Konopka also found few gang girls in her sample of delinquents.

when girls leave. The girl who has learned little of fidelity in personal relationships since childhood expects to be neither the giver nor the receiver of such fidelity. She lives in a power-oriented atmosphere where a bully or boy-snatcher of one week may become a scapegoat the next. A girl usually "plays it cool" and doesn't get too emotionally involved with others.

The supreme master at "playing it cool" is the instigator. She herself refrains from fighting but goads others to fight and is around as an interested spectator at any brawl. She is a rather detached, somewhat psychopathic girl who, without passion but with much malice aforethought, can calmly and collectedly throw others to the lions. Her style of instigating varies in different circumstances. When she sees her own worst self in an infantile girl who whines hysterically after a quarrel with her only friend, the instigator moves in, pulls the whiner's skirt, pokes her, then deftly withdraws. The instigator may be angry at the world in general. When a fight is brewing, she encourages the bully, makes derogatory comments about the victim, and calls the girls to watch. By instigating, a girl can have it both ways: she can "keep out of trouble" and she can also have her aggressions aired.

Even in the most power-oriented group a girl may play a role, such as that of supporter, that is not at all power-oriented. When somebody seems despondent, the supporter calms her. When a girl is demeaned by her peers and pushed from the room, she calls her back. And when another wants to go to a dance, she borrows a dress for her and helps her to get ready. The supporter, though she may be desperately seeking after love, performs an assertive, kindly role. Since the foundations for such a role are shaky, she does not maintain this positive performance under stress but then becomes an agitator or bully.

The bully-flunky interaction underpins the two delinquent groups that were observed. One group, which is blatantly anti-authority, has re-created its delinquent way of life within the hospital walls, sometimes even aided and abetted by the attendants. The attendant staff may tacitly condone the bully role, utilizing the bully for their own purposes, as a protection if they are afraid of the girls, or as a "strong arm" to get the girls to do their bidding.

A tall, broad-shouldered bully orders the girls, at the attendant's behest, to get in line for lunch. Other bullies bring back an obstreperous girl who refuses to have her nails cut by the attendant. The girls in this power-oriented delinquent group indicate that adults, by virtue of being adults, are never on their side. At best there can be a truce with adults, but during periods of tension the alignment becomes clear-cut.

In the second group, where the human surroundings are more benevolent and stimulating, the bully-flunky interaction is more covert, coming out into the open only during periods of tension. A hard-working psychiatric nurse and psychiatrist try to develop each girl's competence, whether in dance, art, or baby-tending. The nurse is an educator and leader, with a whimsy, a vivacity, and a rebellious spirit that is very appealing to the girls. She guides and cajoles and humors and reprimands her charges during her nine-to-ten-hour work day. Many of the girls come and go from her office all during the day. "Can I make you coffee?" "May I clean your desk?" "What can I do?" Or, "May I talk with you?" they ask. The girls give the nurse a surprise party as she has done for each of them. Though an occasional attendant is regarded by the girls as hostile, there is little derogation of the attendants generally. A camaraderie sometimes develops between girl and attendant and attendants may become play mothers for the girls. (Little of this, however, carries over after the nurse's departure. I revisited this ward long after the "good authority," the active charge nurse, has left. The girls' lips have become redder, their dresses tighter, their hair blonder and curlier. They seem now to need this accentuation of feminine physical characteristics to provide some assurance, however bleak, of their existence as persons.)

Sexual forays are often conducted in a context of power plays and counterplays. The most valuable possession that a girl can acquire is a boy. One girl often accuses another of snatching this valuable prey.

The sexual power game is two-pronged. It involves power over boys and, in consequence, power over other girls. "Don't take him from me," one girl implores, and another retorts somewhat mildly, "I will if I want him." A girl's ultimate bargaining instrument in this power game is her body. Through withholding her body she can achieve control over the boy. Through surrendering her body she can win a little friendship and favor. It is a game which enthralls her and possesses her.

The delinquent girls in the hospital come predominantly from the lower class, where the direct expression of power and aggression is more acceptable than in the middle class. The middle-class girls in the group also participate in the power-oriented interaction. Again, how much this kind of relation is endemic to the lower class, to the delinquent, or to both, is not clear.

THE "POPULAR" GIRL VS. THE "IDEAL" GIRL

The sexual sophisticate is accorded popularity and prestige by her delinquent peers. Five of the six most popular girls in one of the delinquent groups are regarded as sexual sophisticates.[6] The popular sexual sophisticate is the highest authority on most matters crucial to the group. She usually possesses a high degree of toughness and boldness as well as wit and skill in boy-girl banter. Though she is often unscrupulous and abides by no rules in her seizure of men, she displays a live–let-live attitude in other spheres and does not resort to bullying.

Sally, by far the most popular member of the group, has been sexually promiscuous since she was eleven. She doles out advice from her vast experience. She tells Felicia that she is very innocent, she is still a virgin. "I'm a virgin," admits Felicia. "But I'm not so innocent. I lived with a man who molested me." Sally laughs. "You don't know what 'molested' means. You think if a man puts his hand up you, it's molesting you." Felicia admits this is true. "You're just fourteen," says Sally. "You're a baby yet. Give yourself time." Sally concedes that she is just a year older but she has had lots of experience.

[6] When the girls rate HOW EACH OF THE OTHER GIRLS IS on the dimension of sexuality-relations with boys, whether (1) sexy, boy-crazy; (2) likes to be with boys; (3) bashful, shy with boys; or (4) keeps away from boys, the six most popular girls get a mean rating of (1.8).

Sally is not popular with the attendants, who speak of her with aversion when they are interviewed at the conclusion of the study.

Sally is impossible. There is nothing you can get her to do for you. She tells the girls pretty fabulous stories.

She is a ringleader and the girls follow her. They say that her mother is a prostitute, that she taught her the ropes.

She can tell things so, her sex experiences. She always has a group of girls around her. She is smart and tricky like.

She is always talking about boys. She shares her cigarettes and her money with the girls and she helps them with their hair styles.

The adults seem to reiterate that Sally's popularity and her power over the group depend largely upon her wit, her boldness, her friendliness with peers, and her aura of sexual sophistication.

Though the most popular girls in the group are often seen as "sexy and boy-crazy," yet girls speak in deprecating terms when they are asked, in the abstract, to describe the "sexy and boy-crazy" girl.

They're too crazy about boys. They act too phony with them, as though it's the only thing they need in this world. They say, "I would like to live with a boy." They would die if they didn't have them around.

They show off in front of a guy, shake all around.

They like to hug up on a boy all the time.

If they don't have the boys on the ward, they go crazy.

The delinquent's ideal girl is the sweet, shy maiden who doesn't let the boys "get her into trouble." When the girls rate how they WOULD LIKE TO BE, whether (1) sexy, boy-crazy; (2) likes to be with boys; (3) bashful, shy with boys; or (4) keeps away from boys, the group mean is (2.6). This is far away from "sexy, boy-crazy" and closer to the category, "bashful, shy with boys." The discrepancy between the attributes of the popular girl (1.8) and the attributes of the ideal girl (2.6) suggests an ambivalence with regard to desirable sexual behavior.

The kindly and noncompetitive girl is often popular in the delinquent group provided she does not allow herself to become a scapegoat or flunky. High status is thus given to the less assertive girl who may be seen through delinquent eyes as resembling in some fashion the ideal girl.

The delinquent maintains that she likes to see herself as a good girl (the ideal girl) who is modest in her relations with boys and gives little of herself sexually beyond a peck on the cheek. She is a virgin, one girl affirms, and won't get involved with her brother's friends when they make up to her. (This girl becomes sexually provocative in her dress, her gait, and her manner in the presence of boys.) Another girl reads aloud from the article, "Good Girls Do Pet," in *Personal Romances:* "Twenty percent of fourteen-year-old girls have indulged in petting." "This isn't true," she asserts indignantly. She reads on: "Among girls fifteen to seventeen, one-third reported petting to some extent." "This isn't true either," she protests. (Now fourteen and indignant about statistics on petting, she was brought to court by her mother for sexual promiscuity at the age of twelve.)

In her choice of paintings to hang on the wall of her bedroom, she is likely to choose religious subjects if they are available, but never a nude. "That one's nasty," she exclaims as she points to a painting of a nude woman. "That's not nasty," she is corrected by one of her more knowledgeable peers. "That's art."

SUBSTITUTE GRATIFICATION: PSEUDOFAMILY ROLES

The delinquent girl looks for substitute family relations through playing pseudofamily roles and establishing either a sibling or a parent-child relationship with her peers. A play father "protects" his daughter and doesn't "disown" her. A play mother "takes care of" her daughter and "doesn't let her get into any trouble." But even in play the girl is not optimistic. The play mother who is depressed announces that she "disowns" her children for the day, though she may later rescind the announcement. "Family" relationships are tenuous and roles are uncertain. Girls who are play sisters one week become play mother and play daughter the next, or may even become estranged from one another. "Disowning" is an habitual occurrence in the play-family group,

children disowned by parents and parents by children. This is presumably how the girl has experienced the transience and uncertainty of her own family living.

The pseudofamily relationship she establishes with boys is
openly manipulative. A girl writes a letter to one of her boy friends.
"Tell him to get skirts for his wife and daughter," beseeches her
chums. "No, don't say that. I'm embarrassed," she confesses, but
hastily adds, "Sizes twenty-two and twenty-four. And we must smell
nice. Also some perfume." The adolescent girl who is preoccupied
with pseudofamily roles is looking at the world in terms of a family
—a "father" to protect her, a "mother" to care for her, "sisters and
brothers" to befriend and serve her—the family she did not experience.

Fantasies of motherhood

Cut off from her mother, a girl may fantasy having
babies. Given below is Bobby's involved and prolonged fantasy of
pregnancy. Her mother is now pregnant and also has a little baby.
She has a new life with a new man and Bobby doesn't fit in.

Bobby, a dull-looking, slow-moving fourteen-year-old Negro girl, says
she is worried that she is going to have a baby. She did something one
weekend and she hasn't had her period for six months (later amended to
three months). "Tell me about babies," Bobby implores. "How they come
out. Does it hurt? Where they come from." The father is George who was
in the Army but she thinks is now in jail. She met George in a restaurant
during Easter week. When her uncle went to make a phone call, George
came over and talked to her and asked her to go up to his hotel room. He
was light-skinned and handsome like her father. George told her he loved
her and wanted to marry her. He needed sex because he didn't get any in
the Army, there were only men. He tied her hands behind her and put
his tongue in her mouth. When it was over, he took her back to the
restaurant. This is the only time she saw him. Her mother said she would
kill her if she got pregnant. And her mother means what she says.

She has made a mess of her life. She knows life so early. It will all be
written down in God's book. She has a curse, she's been bad. Men are no
good, they mess a girl's life. But she really does love George. He's so
handsome. He wrote once and she hopes he writes again.

Do I think they will let her keep her baby? She wants to. She knows what to do with it, to burp it. A baby doesn't need a father. I tell Bobby that she couldn't yet know if she were pregnant by George if she just met him Easter week. Bobby laughs and says it must have been Pablo. Pablo was Spanish and dark-skinned like her.

A week later, Bobby again asks me to sit down with her and again asks about babies. I ask why she is so interested and she says she wants one. She can take care of it. She doesn't want to get married. Most men are no good anyway. They beat women and then they go away. Her mother hasn't been here for three weeks. She is punishing Bobby for smoking on the street corner with a boy. Do I think they would let her keep her baby? She could put it in a nursery and go out and work. She thinks about it all the time, she has nothing else to think about.

This girl retreats into her own fantasy world of motherhood. Even with her own child, she makes little reference to personal contact.

SUBSTITUTE GRATIFICATION: "LOST IN THE CROWD"

Life in any delinquent group is impulsive and impetuous and it is likely to be so at the hospital, especially during a period of stress. At this time the girl's indulgence in excitement and thrill comes into full bloom. She engages in no drawn-out soliloquy, no reflective contemplation of whether to act or not to act. Desires and cravings are indulged without weighing consequences. Following such stressful occurrences as staff conflict or change of routine, behavior in a delinquent group whose members are bored and frustrated and without internal resources degenerates into verbal cataclysms (in the first instance cited below) or else into physical violence and near riots (in the "less civilized" second instance). The bully and the scapegoat now appear in pure form.

A new attendant of stern demeanor appears on the ward one afternoon and mutual antipathy quickly develops between her and the charge nurse. The attendant is outraged: one girl wanted to know whether her husband fucks her every night—never has a girl asked her that! This girl was so quiet on the downstairs ward. And the nurse in turn is miffed by the psychiatrist's observation that the ward is becoming a little lax. Either in reaction to the psychiatrist's censure or to the formidable new attendant, the charge nurse orders the girls' rooms locked at a time when they are usually open.

Shortly thereafter, Molly is crying because she can't enter her room and get her books, Vivian sways in her chair, Rachel sits alone weeping, Mary runs back and forth across the room. Though the doors are opened at noon, the tension continues throughout the day. Girls kick one another and throw food at dinner. One girl provokes Molly, an habitual scapegoat, who starts to whine. After dinner Molly is teased some more and continues whining. "That Jew girl," declares one girl. "A fucking Jew," asserts another. "There's Miss Cohen, and she's Jewish," somebody interjects. "Are you?" one girl asks. "I don't mean her, she's nice," explains Betty. "We didn't mean you, only her," reiterates Ann. "I knocked Molly's head in two once, and I can do it again," vows Frances. "She should have more than her head knocked in two," asserts Bernice. "She should have her whole body cut in two, one part going one way, one another," says Ann with finality and she dramatizes as she talks.

The veneer of the girls is easily shattered. With minimal provocation, bitter venom and scapegoating emerge. For the most part the eruption remains on the verbal level and physical violence is not resorted to.

In the following example, the eruption does turn physical. It is visiting day at the hospital. Few of the girls have visitors. Many sit by the locked door waiting expectantly and become increasingly frustrated.

An attendant comes on duty at 4 P.M., turns off the television and announces that since the girls did not act well with the boys this morning, they cannot have a party with them this evening nor can they watch their favorite television program. She knows what the girls do with the boys even though she wasn't here this morning: they grind and they smooch. The girls protest that only two of the girls were doing this in the corners.

The attendant has given an additional insult to a group that is already frustrated by the lack of visitors and bored by the lack of program. In this situation, the girls adopt no patterned roles but instead engage in disorganized mob activity. Zelda drops her tray on the floor. The girls plan vengeance. They will have a pillow fight in the hall. They will have a riot. They will all be lesbians and treat their girl friends as boy friends. Sally dances around with her dress up to her waist and Abby does a strip tease. The girls start throwing chairs and pillows.

A resident psychiatrist enters the dayroom. The girls crowd about her and beg to see the boys tonight. The request is not granted. Next they implore the nurse when she appears on the ward. The order canceling the party is rescinded and the girls go off peacefully to take their showers.

This incident stirs the girls to deliberate chaos. Each girl adds fuel to the flames until the situation reaches riotous proportions.

Outside the hospital the delinquent girl, out of boredom and frustration, readily joins any available group that may offer immediate excitement. A gang of delinquent boys, in its revolt against the authority of parents or school or community, can swiftly rally the girl to its side, though the girl's rebellion against authority in general may not be so acute nor her desire for retaliation so keen. Usually with few inner resources, the girl is open to such a momentarily prestigeful opportunity, and she heedlessly sells her freedom for a fleeting sense of belonging within the retrograde community of delinquent peers.

HER PURSUIT OF LEARNING

In the classroom the delinquent girl shows little tolerance for frustration and an inability to concentrate. She may have some momentary motivation to learn but unless this motivation can be quickly utilized by the teacher, it is lost and the girl's attention is soon diverted.

As part of her spelling lesson, Carmen works industriously for ten minutes copying words from the blackboard into her notebook. Then she writes on her paper, "I dedicate to you 'The Ten Commandments of Love' " and hands the paper to her Play Mother (a classmate).
I help Adele with her arithmetic exercises. She is challenged and writes out exercises to practice on the ward that evening. But the moment of enthusiasm is followed by frustration and Adele tears up the sheet.

A lack of sustained involvement is not found in all delinquent girls. Sally, for instance, practices shorthand on her own and occasionally studies Spanish but, despite her popularity, her activity does not stimulate imitation.

Some of the girls talk about entering evening classes. They seem to feel there will be less competition and less frustration in such classes where they will not have to meet standards, either intellectual or social, that are set by their peers. In addition, attendance at evening classes will help them to "keep out of trouble."

The delinquent girl who is lower class recognizes that she has little chance of exploring any creative potentiality and being "good" at something. Her idealized identity is tied not to a good education and a middle-class job but merely to a modicum of learning together with some moderate respectability in language and manners. Even in this, she senses her deficiency. Her profane language she regards as a badge of as well as a chain to the lower class. When she discovers that her profanity has been taped, she repeats over and over disbelievingly, "I didn't know it was going." [7] She reflects upon her lack of manners at the dinner table. "Do you think we are savages?" asks one girl. "Teach us how to eat," implores another.

THE DELINQUENT HISTORY

Given below are brief histories of three delinquent girls: their abandonment; their confirmation as "bad" by significant others; and their subsequent affirmation through delinquent behavior.

[7] The attendants complain about the girls' obscene language and sometimes react to this language as though it were a very personal affront. Some of them come from families or environments where these obscenities are common. But they regard their jobs, and therefore themselves, as middle class, and the use of profane language, in public at least, they consider a lower-class characteristic that they would like to repudiate.

The teachers at the hospital talk about an attractive white middle-class girl in terms such as these: "She's so much nicer than the girls here." "She doesn't learn anything from mingling here." "She's a pleasure to have around, she's so well-bred."

The middle-class orientation of hospital personnel widens the gap between them and the lower-class girl and impedes mutual understanding. The discrimination by middle-class teachers and administrators against lower-class children was noted by Hollingshead in a small Midwestern community two decades ago. It is not always clear whether such discrimination is due to the class position of the child directly or to her lack of conformity to staff standards. *See* August B. Hollingshead, *Elmtown's Youth* (New York: John Wiley & Sons, Inc., 1949), pp. 163-203.

1. Sally was born when her mother was sixteen and did not want the responsibility of a child. Her father deserted soon after her birth and her mother left shortly thereafter with another man. Sally was cared for by her grandmother. When she was ten, her mother took her to live with her and seemingly encouraged her to have sexual relations with older men who came to the house.

Sally returned to her grandmother but by fourteen she was an "old hand" at sexually promiscuous relations. Discovered with a boy in her room, she was dubbed "bad" ("just like her mother") by her grandmother. She was sent to an institution for delinquent girls, which reinforced her "bad" personification. She ran away and was then sent to a mental hospital.

Sally seems to want to reestablish a relationship with her mother who abandoned her and she tries to utilize all the resources at her disposal in this pursuit. First, "I'll be like my mother," she appears to say. Second, "I'll take care of my mother, I'll become a secretary (instead of the dancer which I know I could be) to help my mother (in the hope that some day she might be a real mother to me)." She studies Spanish, shorthand, and English grammar on the hospital ward. For some extended period she concentrates completely on each subject and then drops it. She envisages the reversal of roles, she becoming the strong "mother" protecting her real mother.

Sally is queen of her peers at the state hospital and she knows superbly well how to get along with these peers. She is very pretty, of superior intelligence, and she identifies completely with the girls against the staff. She is friendly and supportive with her peers and has many sex tales to tell. She has "lived." But she seems tormented by her "bad" personification—her compulsive sexual promiscuity, which brands her an inferior being worthy only of second-rate companions—and also by the fact of having been betrayed by her mother. "Good behavior," she indicates, would involve having "decent" friends—"good people your own age." Being the leader in an "inferior" peer group is not enough. She craves but despairs of achieving acceptance from more accomplished peers of both sexes. When asked to complete the sentence, "Sometimes I feel like . . . ," she adds, "dying," and this feeling seems evidenced by the numerous self-inflicted scars on her body and by her suicide attempts. Her suicidal gestures are indicative of her despair of having any satisfactory relationships. Her suicidal gestures are also cries for help—somebody will "listen" and will resolve her impasse.

Even in her present "rock-bottom" state, Sally seems to have some of the requisites for achieving both autonomy and personal relation. She has a beautiful body and an astute mind and she seems to want to use them both to advantage. "My body—it does what I want it to," she says exultantly, as though, under other circumstances, she is capable of experiencing sexual intimacy in all of its passion. She engages in give-and-take relations with girls on the ward and she immerses herself in her studies, seeming to retain some glimpse of the woman she might be.

2. Lois' early life is characterized by neglect rather than physical abandonment. Lois' mother ousted her father after he was jailed for robbery. Lois indicates that her father was kind to her. Her mother, who attended college, now lives in poverty-stricken surroundings in Harlem, sharing bath and kitchen with other families. She has a boy friend and "when he comes home at night there is arguing, lots of arguing and fights," Lois relates. Lois seems to see this boy friend as an intruder. Her psychological examination indicates some identification with her mother who is perceived as "sexual."

In early adolescence Lois joins a gang in her neighborhood and she soon engages in sex relations. "Look what I'm doing, it's bad and it's what you taught me," she seems to say to her mother. She did gain her mother's attention. Her behavior is declared "bad" by her mother who takes her to court when she is twelve. Her mother blames the "bad company," and Lois concurs. She says she liked to have extra money and all the other girls were doing it. The court confirms that her behavior was bad and it is accepted as such by Lois herself. "I can't help it, that's the way I am," she explains. "You know, I'm a follower. If other kids steal and do other things, I follow them."

Lois has felt the "push" from home and the anticipation of excitement from the "wrong" crowd. She recognizes that she can't go home again—the rivalrous relationship with her mother has become blatant.

She waits week after week for her mother to come to take her from the hospital on a long-delayed home visit. Each weekend she expresses disappointment.

After the visit home, Lois pulls my hair, punches me, and proclaims accusingly, "You are a prostitute." She also is cranky with the girls. What's eating her, I ask. She describes the competitive relationship with her mother. "It's my mother, she was mean to me. People say to her, 'Lois is getting big,' and she answers, 'Not so big that I can't turn her over my knee.' She doesn't like it when people say I am prettier than she is. She used to be a nice mother but she isn't any more. She wouldn't let me go out, she was afraid I would associate with boys."

Lois searches for further relation. We may conjecture that the early good relationship with her father, who was also rejected, and perhaps with her mother too, gives her some emotional base of operation today. She is an outgoing, somewhat boisterous girl who occasionally shows petulance and hostility but is generally friendly with both adults and peers. She is often a leader of her group. Many girls ask her to be their play mother. She is seen by staff as "a normal kid, who will help girls with their assignments if they are tired, who will settle arguments among the girls."

She would like to go somewhere else to live, Lois says, "some place where children go to stay." She is not obsessed with inner torment but seems free to begin again and make a new life.

3. Fay's parents, lower-middle-class Jews, preserve their distance and approach their daughter only to scold and admonish her. She is now an adolescent and their scoldings revolve around the use of her body. The buxom quality of this body, where "everything" shows, adds insult to injury. She becomes the misshapen daughter goaded and stimulated with prohibitions and admonitions, "You're nothing but a prostitute," "You belong on the streets," "Don't you come home with a black child." Her parents are frantic when she leaves the house and when she associates with Negro boys in her racially mixed neighborhood. "She dances like a Negro," they say.

When Fay returns one evening at ten, she is greeted with, "You're going to have a baby, aren't you?"

The best Fay can do to be confirmed in a relation with her detached and forbidding parents is to pit her will against theirs and to become what her mother warns her against.[8] "I wanted to spite my parents, and I was doing it [by truanting and sexual activity]. They made me come home at nine. Other kids my age were allowed out until eleven, so I stayed out too," Fay explains.

Fay is excited temporarily with each new relation with a boy but her elation is quickly followed by depression. In the hospital, where there is little possibility for a sexual relationship, an all-pervasive depression engulfs her. Upon leaving the hospital, she enrolls in business school to become a secretary. But she continues her compulsive search for relation, which in itself precludes establishing a personal relation. Her parents watch circumspectly for some backsliding. Unable to endure the strain, they ask for her readmission to the hospital several weeks after her release.

We may ask: with a background characterized by abandonment —either physical or emotional—why doesn't the delinquent girl give up the search for relation and retreat into solitary autism? Why isn't she "sicker" than she is? We may conjecture that in her earliest years she experienced some tenderness with parent or parental substitute. As an infant she may have been a "doll" to whom a parent could safely show tenderness but as she grew older this avenue was closed. The more frequent the confrontation between parent and child, however carping this confrontation, the more vital and life-preserving the delinquent girl's present search for relation.

---

[8] *See* Adelaide Johnson's development of the thesis that parents often unconsciously encourage a child's delinquent activity. Such activity gives them vicarious gratification of their own poorly integrated forbidden impulses and at the same time enables them to express hostile, destructive feelings toward the child. ("Sanctions for Superego Lacunae of Adolescents," in K. R. Eissler [ed.], *Searchlights on Delinquency* [New York: International Universities Press, 1949], pp. 225-245.)

The parents, then, unconsciously mean the *opposite* of what they say: "Don't" means "do." Whether it is necessary to "read in" this interpretation in this instance is debatable.

EXTENT OF ALIENATION

The girl's "bad" personification is derived from her
experience with a family that abandons and rejects her, and is further confirmed by societal judgment about her deviant status. She
divides people into the "good" and the "bad" and she sees herself
as "bad." She watches the movie, "So Young, So Bad" as it appears
on the television screen each day for a week and she empathizes
with the "bad" characterizations. She discusses what she will do
when she is "free." "I'll go to church every week," vows one girl.
"I'll do more than that," promises another. "I won't have God lose
faith in me."

The delinquent girl does not lash out against a society that has
provided little, and she is not alienated from that society. If she
is institutionalized, she may say, "My mother sent me," or "The
judge sent me," and she may express resentment toward both, but
she usually adds that perhaps they had good cause. "I once stayed
out most of the night, came home drunk, and my mother said she
was going to send me back here. I double-dared her and she did."

The delinquent in the hospital has fears for the future. Can
she be "good" on the outside? Will she be back? The stories that
she reads in her pulp and comic magazines have a recurring theme:
a basically good, decent girl makes some error but things somehow
work out well in the end. The good girl, who is sincere, honest,
hard-working, and something less than beautiful, has misunder-
standings and mishaps, but finally gets her man, marries him, and
presumably lives happily ever after. This is the future she is seeking.

In summary, the delinquent girl has a problem in relation. She
is the girl confirmed as "bad" who lives out her "badness" and
searches for other "bad" companions. As a consequence of the bar-
renness of her early family life, she has little experience in what is
involved in achieving intimacy and love. She requires that someone
be close, that she have a relation at any price, and so she compulsively flees from one relation to another, the flight itself obviating
the possibility of any permanent relation. Since she cannot endure
living outside relation, becoming desperately lonely and depressed,
she has little potentiality for autonomy.

seven

THE ANARCHIC
BOHEMIAN:
HER SEARCH
FOR AUTONOMY

The anarchic bohemian is not driven to look for relations with others, as is the delinquent, but rather, for freedom
from the kind of relation that she knows best and that has been
restrictive and persistent. She wants the freedom to be "herself"
and she sees herself not in relation with people but as an integral
part of the "natural" world. She wants to absorb this world in its
richness and immediacy, undiluted by societal proscriptions. She
wants to express her primitive vitality and thereby experience her
own unique sensuous self. Thus she hopes to find her "kicks" not
through relation but through "losing" or abandoning herself. She
is looking for the heightened perception, the greater awareness,
beyond relation. This is essentially a search for autonomy as an
end in itself.

The description of the anarchic bohemian is complicated by the
fact that: (1) my sample is limited to high school girls, whose turn
toward the anarchic bohemian way of life is not yet necessarily
clear-cut; and (2) the anarchic bohemian may also be delinquent.
In addition to her confirmation as "peculiar," she has also been
confirmed as "bad." Combined with the anarchic bohemian's search
for autonomy is the delinquent's search for relation.

HOW MUCH AUTONOMY?

The anarchic bohemian immerses herself in music and
art and roams widely in literature. She writes poetry, essays, and
short stories, and is skilled in the performing arts.

Though she pursues one intellectual diversion after another and
speaks well the language of the intellect and the arts, she usually
possesses only the trappings of knowledge. To withdraw from relations and undertake autonomous pursuits, one must feel secure
in relations with others. Otherwise, one is likely to engage only in
anxious grasping and not in any sustained endeavor. The anarchic
bohemian lacks security in her relations with others. Her consequent vacillation in matters artistic and intellectual and her lack
of rigorous self-discipline preclude intensive probing. Combined
with her lack of sustained involvement is often an intellectual as-
tuteness. She is the Brain and the Free Thinker described below.
Her frustration is deeper than the delinquent's because her initial
sights are set higher. She experiences more detachment and self-
awareness, and therefore probably more despair.

She stabs mercilessly at her family's and society's hypocrisies
and derides their overemphasis on materialism. In all of this she
has nothing of the social critic or the social missionary about her
but rather she is the anarchic rebel who defies in a detached, isolated way without seeking followers. Abhorring materialism and
bureaucracy, she turns disdainfully from all of the prevailing institutions and values. "What they're for, I'm against," is her byword. Her separatism is a permanent retreat rather than a temporary retrenchment. Genuine autonomy presupposes a return to
satisfactory relation. The anarchic bohemian engages only in
pseudoautonomy.

HOW MUCH RELATION?

The anarchic bohemian pattern sets a premium on
withdrawal as a way of life—primarily withdrawal from the larger
community, but also to some degree withdrawal within the group
itself.

The bohemian may join a group of her peers and gravitate with them to defined areas of the city. She engages in philosophic and aesthetic and psychological "talk" and she may (or may not) maintain heterosexual contact. But she is likely to be a social isolate. She doesn't need people, all she needs is a library, one bohemian confesses in a moment of self-pity. She may be agonized by her own failure to feel deeply about others. "I intermingle and then I mangle," is another self-characterization.

She is oriented largely to her own comfort. Her deep, brooding, depressive self-involvement interferes with her peer relations. In seeking to "live fully," she often indulges her whims, with little regard for consequences to herself or for the interests and convenience of others. She stays away from home overnight and on her return is ecstatic in her description of the beauty of the sunrise, without concern for the furor she has aroused. She practices her modern dance while her employer waits.

In her sexual relations, she usually considers herself a free thinker unimpeded by societal proscription. She may go farther than her conforming peers, though, only in her talk. Or, like the delinquent, she may flee from one man to another, seeking to abandon herself in the sensuous moment.

The anarchic bohemian does have clinging relationships with other persons but, as with the delinquent, there is no trust of others and the relationships don't last. She is "peculiar," she is "uniquely different," this is now her character (see the histories below), and she fears rejection from others because of it.

THE BOHEMIAN PATTERN AT THE PRIVATE HOSPITAL

The bohemian pattern emerges as one framework in which to look at the girls at the private hospital. Representative roles are the detached rebel, the brain, and the free thinker. The pattern is not always seen in clear focus at the hospital because it is attenuated by the intensive program of psychotherapy, occupational therapy, recreation, and school; and it is diluted by the presence of some adolescents whose values are the antithesis of bohemian. The pattern emerges more clearly when several girls are followed after they leave the hospital.

The detached rebel

A characteristic role among the anarchic bohemians is the detached rebel, whose rebellion takes place along many fronts: against peer group, staff, family, school, sex mores, and social ideology.

Ruth, the group's detached rebel, is steeped in her own problems and often ignores the interests and desires of her peers. She plays the piano very loudly and very well, oblivious to whether she is disturbing others. She prints "Harold" in large letters over the group mural, then draws on the mural in unrelated fashion, and the group spends a long and frustrating time trying to erase the damage. She seems to be expressing contempt for these peers.

Her dress sets her apart from other girls. She often appears in nondescript blue jeans with unironed shirt or else in a seductive, tight-fitting dress and high-heeled shoes. "Your fine feathers are sham and pretense," she is saying. "Let's get back to what counts. I shall use my 'femininity' to achieve my ends." Her hair is long and straggly. (Is cleanliness sterility for her and dirt, earthiness?)

She makes her own rules and regulations. She shoplifts at the commissary. (If she can't give to the poor, she can at least take from the rich.) She fails a regents' examination in defiance of an educational system that teaches too little. She runs away from the hospital. When her peer repeats the administrator's warning of discharge for running away, Ruth announces, "That's what he told me the first time I ran away, and the second. He didn't mention it the third." She can safely test the limits, for she is willing to endure the consequences: to live outside the relation.

She often rebels against the lower-staff authority: against the big, burly attendant who brings her back early from the evening activity and against the attendant who refuses her request for bread before lunch.

She seeks freedom from all familial control. Her rejection of her family's values is manifested in her sexual promiscuity, her involvement with a noneducated, non-Jewish boy, and her "block" in school. Indiscriminately she breaks the idols that her family worships: sexual restraint, respectability in dress, responsibility, self-discipline, and hard work.

Ruth herself poses the question: autonomy for what? Is she merely the stubborn, rebellious dissident, she wonders, or the potential innovator? When she expresses disagreement at home, her mother says to her in derision, "Everybody's out of step but Ruth!" But maybe Ruth is right. Maybe everybody else IS out of step, she muses. Galileo was discussed in class today. He thought the earth was round when nobody else did. Should he have kept quiet? For the moment, she sees her search for autonomy in the best possible light. She sees herself as an independent human being, creating as she wishes.

After leaving the hospital, Ruth continues her rebellion along all fronts, though she does graduate from high school. She tours the country with one man or another, then returns to New York and joins a group of Beat artists and writers. In her numerous jobs she seems to expect that her superior comprehension and her facile articulateness will enable her to accomplish the work assigned in half the time required. Her selective inattention to work instruction seems to indicate a rebellion against the authority imposing such instruction. The middle-class world owes her an easy living, this brilliant young woman seems to feel. She thus knocks over yet another standard in her anarchic flight from authority into a pseudoautonomy.

The brain

In the bohemian framework, a girl should have at least the trappings of intellectual sophistication. The brain is, consequently, an esteemed role.

Ruth, the detached rebel, is also the brain. She seems to know most of the intellectual answers. She reads widely and tries to write. She is skilled in many areas: at the piano, as a poet, in arts and crafts. She likes to play with ideas.

But the brain among the bohemians lacks the self-discipline to sustain any long-range commitment to intellectual and aesthetic concerns.

The free thinker

The free thinker exhibits the anarchic bohemian's
search for autonomy in her restless pursuit of one intellectual diversion after another and in her critical, "free-thinking" approach.

Betty, the free thinker, displays a wide range of knowledge and
experience. "That's part of her illness," observes one of her peers,
"to act as though she knows it all." Betty discourses glibly on such
diverse topics as Japan's houses of prostitution, the meetings of
world leaders, and the exotic food that she has prepared or eaten.
She exhibits a piece of sculpture and assiduously describes her
handiwork: a pregnant woman with very large protuberances, with
one breast missing, a distorted back, and a "bi-sexual" face. The
features of the male side are clear and differentiated, says Betty,
as is man's role in our society. The female features are not in so
good a perspective, according to Betty, though the features seem
very sharp to the observer.

Betty acts the free thinker not only in matters intellectual and
artistic but also in matters of sex. She confesses that she was fitted
for a diaphragm and instructs one of her peers in the art of combining the roles of mistress and college student. "Even if it's not
for love," explains Betty, "he can make it worth your while."

The free thinker is searching for "what she is meant to be."
Her search is very different from the more mundane search of the
adolescent girl who expresses the desire for a man, marriage, and
family. Betty sees herself at various times as a ravishing, sophisticated female or else as a Zen Buddhist, an anarchist, a critic of
United States foreign policy, a searcher for an atman, and a talented
artist. She has not yet found a niche of her own. She admits sometimes that she is "whistling in the dark," but she feels that her
free-thinking role gives her some status in the interim period when
she "doesn't know where she's going." "You are the inferior one,"
she seems to be saying. "You who can't see beyond your primary
relations. I may be foundering, but I'm reaching for the stars."

Given below are brief histories of two anarchic bohemians
found at the hospital. The first is Ruth, described above as the

detached rebel and the brain, the second is Betty, described above
as the free thinker.

HER CONFIRMATION BY PARENTS:
THE ANARCHIC BOHEMIAN HISTORY

1. Ruth comes from a lower-middle-class family. Her
father is a watchmaker, skilled in his trade, her mother, a librarian. The parents' middle-class values are rigidly and undeviatingly
maintained. The household is conventional and leaves little opportunity for fun and self-directed adventure. There is constant
battle between Ruth's domineering, shrewish mother and her passive though sometimes tempestuous and rageful father.

Ruth's mother is a large, buxom woman who gives one the
initial impression of beneficence. She quickly reveals herself as
tightly wound as her own closely set gray hair. I conjecture that
she is frustrated by her own conventional living, her own lack
of courage and adventure, and that she covertly pushes her daughter
to such adventure, though knocking her down as soon as she ventures forth.[1]

Her father is a rigid man who sticks to his watchmaking and
interferes in the mother-daughter interplay only on occasion when,
for example, he forbids her to read Voltaire or *The Canterbury
Tales,* the latter because some disparaging remark is made about
Jews. Her grandmother Ruth sees as a kind and nonpressuring
woman who gives her the "right" gift, unlike her mother, who
"thrusts everything down her throat."

Until high school, Ruth complied perfectly with her mother's
orders. She obtained excellent grades in school, came home precisely
at the specified time, and thought her parents all-knowing. She
read extensively, wrote poetry, and lived in a world of fantasy.
She dressed primly and sensibly. She was painfully shy with her
peers and had few friends, attending those school dances that were
mandatory. She felt humiliated in her isolation.

[1] Adelaide Johnson's thesis that parents often unconsciously encourage the
girl's deviant activity may apply here. *See* p. 94.

But she was never acceptable to her mother. She was confirmed by her mother as uniquely different, as "peculiar." Her looks were peculiar, her manner was odd, even her awards at school never pleased her mother. When she telephoned her mother from the house of a girl friend and asked if she could accept the invitation to dinner, her mother countered with, "You're lying, she wouldn't invite you to dinner." She was the ugly duckling who came out of the egg in distorted fashion. She was the laughing stock.

At thirteen, Ruth begins to rebel. She truants, stays away from home overnight, and becomes very critical of her mother. Her mother takes her to court and informs the judge that Ruth is a tramp and will come to no good. Hurling accusations of blatant promiscuity, she accuses her daughter of being "morally and sexually depraved." Ruth is confirmed not only as uniquely different and peculiar but also as the enemy whom her mother is out to destroy. Her mother seems to see Ruth as a malevolent person disturbing her own well-being. Ruth's father remains passive through these successive crises though he sometimes exhibits toward her an explosive and sadistic temper.

The court adjudicates Ruth a delinquent. She comes to the hospital and continues her denunciation of her mother. She leads her peers in a song in which a girl brutally exterminates her family. She sees her mother a "master of sarcasm" and a "sick" woman. Her younger sister, she says, has done better than she but is an ingratiator, a "good girl," and Ruth doesn't respect her for that.

Ruth is the group's detached rebel and the brain, whose behavior is often erratic and lacking in self-discipline. She has been confirmed as queer or uniquely different and she affirms herself thus in good measure. She flaunts every rule that the authorities, and even her peers, espouse.

Will she ever achieve self-discipline? She thinks so. When she has children, she says, she will go back to school and become an old-lady librarian (as is her mother) or a social worker. Her establishment of a relationship with children of her own must precede her pursuit of competence, she seems to say. She may be saying too that she can establish a relationship only with children and not with a man, that the best she can hope for is some measure of autonomy but probably very little personal relation. In the meantime, after leaving the hospital, she "loses herself" in undisciplined fashion among a group of bohemian peers.

2. Betty comes from a middle-class family. Her father was an engineer for a large company and was off on business trips for long periods of time; "I never knew where he went." Her mother worked as a dancer for a time on the fringe of bohemia, and turned to secretarial work after marriage. Relations between mother and father were bad, her mother constantly derogating her father. "She made him feel like an outsider," Betty explains.

Her mother, a somewhat unconventional woman who was disdainful in her relations with others, "pushed and pushed" to develop and overdevelop Betty's natural precocity. Betty was the good student who talked glibly, almost like an adult, when still a young child, and who painted and danced early and well. Betty was confirmed early in her precocity, as uniquely different.

Betty speaks about her father's sexual seductiveness and assaultiveness. She took showers with him and engaged in some sex play with him, she says. She expresses resentment toward both parents but especially toward her father.

Her relations with peers have never been good. She feels she never belonged with the crowd. Her sarcasm toward other girls is not veiled. She "loves the monotony of Ina's voice." She "pats Lois' back to make her feel like one of us," then "pukes" when she is away from her. She insults one of her less intelligent roommates; "It really hurts," says this roommate. When she is elected president of the group, a role of some prestige, she displays none of this sarcasm.

In her early teens, Betty rebels against her family. She starts truanting, running away, and having sexual relations with boys.

An exhibitionistic girl, she often walks around in the nude. She parades into the dining room in a pair of natural-colored tights and a shirt of the same color, to the consternation of the other girls. She wears a black sheath dress when the other girls don summer cottons.

She discourses in intellectual clichés about all possible matters, dispensing her vast information in a condescending manner. She reads *Candide* and *Ulysses* while other girls are perusing simpler fare. She delves into the intricacies of Zen Buddhism; her mother is an agnostic and so is she, she explains. In school she finds it difficult to concentrate for long on any subject.

She seems to be affirming herself in the manner she was confirmed: as the precocious girl, several cuts above all of her peers, who must search for the esoteric, since she can never be "one of them."

The characterization of the anarchic bohemian does not fit all bohemians in time or place nor all girls who are perceived as bohemian today. The anarchic bohemian can be contrasted, for example, to Britain's Angry Young Men who, as social reformers, did not reject their world in the same totalistic fashion; or to an earlier era's Angry Young Women, who defied the rules through epic novels that served as "vehicles for spiritual iconoclasm and social rebellion." [2] Such modes of passionate conviction seem unavailable to the girl in anarchic revolt.

[2] Ellen Moers, "The Angry Young Women," *Harper's* (December 1963), pp. 88-95.

eight

THE
AUTONOMOUS
GIRL

The girl described as autonomous is a self-directed girl
who can withdraw from others, both physically and psychologically,
can think and feel for herself, and gains some competence in areas
of interest through her sustained endeavor. She rejoins others,
richer because of her autonomous pursuits; richer also because of
her long beginnings in personal relations. The girl who affirms herself in a personal, genuine manner was confirmed in genuine fashion, as she was, from her earliest years.

HER CONFIRMATION BY PARENTS

The autonomous girl indicates that her parents provide a nonthreatening, nonpressuring haven. "My mother seems to
enjoy my friends and my sister's friends more than adults. It's very
hard to shock her. It's easy for me to entertain at home. Kids can
smoke and talk with her." "My parents brought us up to learn.
They're so nice about marks. They know I can't try any harder.
They say nothing about having to go to a 'good college.'" She
recognizes that her mother is often a convenient scapegoat for her
own frustration. "I get tense so easily with so much work. I take
it out on my mother. When she says, 'Clean up your room' I ex-
plode." Beyond and deeper than her parents' love conditioned on
accomplishment, she senses an unconditional love and acceptance.

Her "good family" is thus good to go back to. "If somebody asked me where I wanted to go most, I'd say home."

The "good family" of the autonomous girl is also good to start out from. Her parents encourage any new venture that she wants to pursue. They introduced her at an early age to many varied experiences—either through the special school and camp she attended or through the parents themselves: their interests, involvements, and desires for their children. "Any interest I've expressed my family has always encouraged me to pursue." "My mom and I have a lot of activities in common. We make our own clothes. She is interested in the theater to some extent, as I am." "In our house, there's a respect for each person as an individual." "Your parents are generally with it to allow kids to travel long distances. It takes an awful lot."

Her mother is described as "honest, efficient, and sincere. She knows what she likes and doesn't like." "She's warm." "She's interested in things. I admire her intelligence and humor. She's a good person."

She mentions the stabilizing influence of her father as well as her mother. Her parents are models of stability alone and also as a pair. Both parents are seen as responsible and self-sufficient and give her the comfortable feeling that they can "handle things." "If the necessity should come for one of my parents to operate without the other, it would be possible." They provide for the daughter whatever stability derives from a happy marriage. "My parents get along very well. My father loves my mother and she loves him. They are always off on trips together or to dinner or the theater. At night, they have cocktails. We stay away. My mother admires my father to death. When she goes out with him, she dresses like a big date, as though they were going steady. And my mother gets prettier and prettier."

She is not the "good girl" who always does what her mother sees as right. Some autonomous girls express a strong desire for independence from parents. "Sometimes you want to be left alone. Your mother doesn't want to leave you alone." "She is too much influenced by some ridiculous ideas of the last century. If I am unchaperoned when I'm baby-sitting, she is likely to say, 'What will the neighbors think—not that I don't trust you.' It doesn't hang together." "Last year my mother was trying to make me into what she is. Nothing specific. She realized she was still treating me at fifteen as at fourteen. Now I'm allowed to do as I please but my mother trusts me. I have no curfew but I have safety restrictions." "She nags me—for instance when I go to bed at 12:30."

Some indicate difficulties communicating with their mothers. "I'd probably be embarrassed confiding in her. I tell my girl friends or nobody." "I don't ask my parents for advice, ever. I usually don't tell them about what I'm doing in school or about boys—only such things as what I should wear or write." "My mother says I don't tell her anything. I think I do. My uncle tells her she isn't supposed to be a pal." "There are things I wouldn't tell my mother—for instance, girls switching their friendships from one to another, or about boys." "She asks me questions that are so guarded and coy. She takes an attitude of a social worker with me when I confide. She doesn't use her maternal instincts." Presumably the dissonance with mother is temporary with the girl who has had a good relationship with her mother during her early years. As a fledgling adolescent (and even earlier), she may set up her mother as a straw man to be torn down so she can feel free to affirm herself in her own personal manner.

In contrast, other autonomous girls say, "I discuss intimate things with both mother and dad. We're interested in one another." "I talk about personal things with my mother, a lot more than to girl friends because I know they won't go any further."

The autonomous girl does not want to pattern herself after her mother, at least not in any one-to-one manner. Though she is fond of her mother and recognizes the security and stability that she provides, she sometimes expresses disappointment that her mother isn't the perfect instrumental model.

Frequently the girl is critical that her mother doesn't utilize her many talents. "She's much too restricted by her own feelings of inadequacy. She was third in her class at college, she can write and organize things, but she hasn't worked since marriage. She doesn't do half of what she can do." "She's very good and doesn't use it at all." [1] She often sees her mother as a "good sort" who stays at home and has never been anywhere or experienced excitement, adventure, or romance, and may therefore be found wanting as a guide worthy of emulation.

Some autonomous girls are critical of their parents' undercommitment. "My parents have settled into a middle-class oblivion. They'd work for organizations if I asked them to but not on their own. Sometimes I feel they're not aware or don't care. But that's bad to say." "My mother believes there's a great deal of Communism in CORE. She wanted me to drop out. I don't know and don't care." "My father doesn't believe in fighting for causes as I do. He says he doesn't think he'd be that brave in any situation. I think he would. He tries to discourage me. It bothers me."

Other autonomous girls are critical of their mothers' oversubscription. "People say she's self-righteous. She doesn't see two sides of it sometimes. She can't stand hypocrisy—people who will go only half-way for a cause." "I think she goes to extremes about civil rights and integration. I'm for equal rights and integration but she's freer than I. She lets herself go more. Sometimes I don't feel it's appropriate."

In the minority are the mothers who appear either under- or overinvolved with their daughters. "She's busy a lot with the library and bookkeeping and playing mahjong. Our paths don't cross very often," one girl muses. "I don't discuss anything of a personal nature with her. Maybe it's something you start when you're very young." Or, "It's my glory," protests the frustrated daughter whose opinions her mother devalues and whose achievements her mother regards as her own. "When I play my composition at the recital, I don't want her there." This mother may be frustrated by her own or her husband's lack of attainment and may attempt to compensate for her failure through her daughter. The latter does not submissively follow the path her mother has laid out and does not become an extension of her mother. I conjecture that these girls had some other important adult influence at an early age.

---

[1] On the other hand, "My parents never stop learning," a girl says with admiration. "My father studied French all last year and my mother, drama and stained glass."

More often than other girls, the autonomous girl has a father who places his distinctive stamp on the development of her autonomy and her relations. He seems often to be a strong father who, cutting the cord between mother and child, encourages his daughter to emulate his own ventures into the world.[2] She sometimes sees herself as resembling her father. "In many ways I'm like him. He always does what he thinks is best."

The autonomous daughter—more than any other—expresses fondness, admiration, and devotion for her father. "My father has so many qualities I want in a husband," one worried daughter confesses. "And he married my mother who is so different from me."

The father, through his responsibility and courage, ensures family stability and security. He "never bends with the breeze but stands up to things. He may be the only one in his neighborhood with his political views but he goes out and talks to people."

The father's prime virtue is involvement with his family. "He's a family man. He listens to us and he discusses everything with us. I don't talk to my mother but to my father or sister. He's not obsessed with having a big car or a big house and he never plays bridge or golf. Instead, he likes rowing or walking—the outdoors. He likes books, likes us, likes to play with us." "We're as close as we can be. He's very quiet and until this year I was too. I don't confide in him though." "He's a good father and a good husband, very good to get along with. If I have problems—I'm not doing well or am having trouble with a subject—I go to him."

HOW MUCH AUTONOMY?

The autonomous girl wants to mold her own life, and she does this, so far as is feasible. Her desire for self-determination is stronger than any urge to conform with peers, parents, or teachers. She refuses to be pressured by others into certain involvements

[2] Ellen Moers, in her article "The Angry Young Women," notes that during the Victorian era a majority of the successful literary rebels she discusses lost their mothers, or came under the dominant influence of fathers, at an early age (for example, the Brontës, Harriet Beecher Stowe, George Eliot, Elizabeth Barrett, and Virginia Woolf) (*Harper's* [December 1963], pp. 88-95).

and she does not rebel against others through her involvements. "Man makes himself," she insists. "You're the one who patterns your own life. No one else has the right to do this."

She contrasts her own optimism that she can "make use of her life and abilities" with the defeatist feeling that a girl can't be autonomous, that she can't escape her environment. "A lot of Negroes have the feeling that everyone is against them and that they are destined to amount to very little," one upper-middle-class Negro girl maintains. "They become conditioned to hopelessness and really think they're inferior. I've never believed that. I never wanted to be anybody's maid or dishwasher. Bigger, in Richard Wright's *Native Son,* thought he could get back at others that way." [3] The cards may be stacked against her, this girl recognizes —and through active participation in the civil rights movement she does what she can to mitigate this—but she insists that each person bears the responsibility to be, so far as possible, the master of her own fate.[4]

The autonomous girl is saying initially, for her future perspective, that she can live outside relation. Camus' *The Stranger* "doesn't feel any loneliness," she says. "Man's total lack of involvement with others eliminates a lot of the pain and the hurt in human relations. Little hurts you get when you care for someone and they don't care for you." She notes the pleasurable escape from people that movies affords. "It can be very personal and vivid, and you forget yourself. Though it's very comforting, it's another form of estrangement."

She has a strong sense of wanting to protect herself, her privacy, and her pride from the pressures of her world. "You sometimes get discouraged by all the work, all the pressures, tests all the time, so much competition for grades. After all that, when you get a letter, 'We sincerely regret to inform you . . . ,' you wonder, what's wrong with you?" "Holden's adults don't quite get the picture, with their

[3] This girl would disagree with the analysis given by one of her peers: "*Native Son* showed why Negroes *are forced* to do things sometimes—constantly *being made* to feel you're not as good" (italics mine).

[4] This statement clearly comes from a girl who has not been severely deprived economically and socially, though she is Negro. Her world has not been one of minimal choice.

pressures to work hard, not shirk duty, be a buddy to you. Why don't they all go away sometimes? Salinger understands, and he's thirty-five at least."

She demands that she be the arbiter of her own thought. She zealously guards her freedom to question and to doubt. "My counsellor at camp couldn't see why I should question rules. She wrote that I was 'too independent'; she wanted 'togetherness.' I didn't want to feel allegiance to the cabin every night. To me, independence is the best thing you can have. Many kids at camp were shocked that I believe in evolution. They never thought of doubting before."

Knowing her own feelings is vital to her. She wants to be sure she isn't merely aping others. "Before reading Langston Hughes I had always discussed what I *read* about the state of my race and not what I *felt*," she confesses. "I never reflected upon it. I was never personally aware."

She places much importance on the authenticity of her feelings which she believes derive from personal experience. "There's as much to do in Harlem as in Mississippi," says one girl who hopes to work in the South when she is self-supporting. "But I'd like to know what it's like in Mississippi. There's only so much you can read about."

She is saying, very self-consciously at this stage, "I want to determine my life at each level of my living."

She wants the freedom to choose her friends for what they are and not because they belong to an in-group—"girls who enjoy the same things, who share my interests," "who have something to them so you want to know them as persons." She doesn't want to "lose herself" in any group.

"I went to Beat parties last year," says one autonomous girl. "There was lots of folk music and folk dancing. They were artificial and superficial— the long hair, long earrings, Greek bangs. I felt myself losing my personal identity, becoming like everybody else in the group. I'm getting away from them."

She is beginning to detach herself from "best" girl friends. "In eleventh grade you're more mature, more independent. No one cares that much about a best friend any more."

In her sexual relations too, her decisions are not determined by peers or by parents. "I've always set my own standards. I've not done what others have done."

In her activities, the autonomous girl conveys something of the artist's creed as expressed by Otto Rank. "The artist needs his calling for his spiritual existence. . . . His calling is life itself." [5] Her "calling" may not be the same in another five years; even now she may disperse her vast energies among several "callings." But she gives herself with zest and exuberance—whether to academic studies, painting, music, or civil rights. She is the thinker who reads extensively and critically, seeking knowledge for its own sake, for the sheer love of understanding and the enrichment of self. She is also the activist who participates in a variety of movements out of a firm sense of her own values.

She may seek to develop competence and mastery as a painter, writer, or actress. Even now, she writes poetry and short stories, submits her writings for publication, and rewrites. She is not foreclosing the choices open to her. "I want to get a liberal arts education," one prospective actress explains. "Anything you can bring to acting from other fields will enrich you. The theater, though, is not a hard-and-fast thing with me. Through exposure to other things, my interests may change."

She is usually committed to school activities. She often edits the literary magazine or school newspaper and participates in the drama club or the foreign policy club. "She does things of special interest to her and she is finding out about herself by doing it," is one girl's analysis. "She is vibrant and committed to whatever comes along." In all of her activity she displays initiative and industry.

She sees her intellectuality generally as an asset in her school environment. "People who are concerned with ideas find themselves more at ease when they have to express themselves," claims one autonomous girl. "Girls don't try to hide their intellect." "She can discuss a subject intelligently, use words properly. She knows good poets. She doesn't choose poetry because it fits into a certain groove,"

[5] Otto Rank, *The Myth of the Birth of the Hero and Other Writings,* Philip Freund (ed.) (New York: Vintage Books, 1959), p. 190. Taken from *Art and Artist* (New York: Alfred A. Knopf, Inc., 1932).

asserts another autonomous girl whose own living room is strewn with books on poetry. Moreover, "It's much easier to develop social graces than intellectual graces," says a girl who has both. A few autonomous girls give more qualified opinions about the social advantages of being intellectual: "It's something added on the plus side, but you shouldn't carry it to the extreme." "A boy won't refuse to ask a girl out if she gets better grades."

In evaluating the Beatniks, the autonomous girl is more sympathetic than is the peer- or the adult-oriented girl. She indicates her preference for individualism over conformity. "I think we need nonconformists." "There are the real Beats and the phony Beats. The phony Beats must cover up their own weaknesses. I don't know the real Beats." "They're usually interested in the arts and literature. They're very liberal-minded, don't tend to discriminate against people. They should be allowed to be different. Before it became a fad, the people were individualized and had the courage to stand up for their convictions." "They're classified in this way much too often. I've been called a Beatnik. Maybe many are sick, maybe they can find out about themselves by being that way. If she becomes a Beat because her friends are, then she's not a Beatnik if this means individualism."

Although she has insisted on self-determination, she speculates on where social and cultural determinism ends and individual freedom begins. She has been stirred by the writings of Sartre and Camus and by what she knows of Existentialism. She mentions Ayn Rand. "Reading her was something new. The feeling of the superiority of self above everything else. It has its limitations and its dangers." She wonders whether freedom for the individual, even in the best sense, is sometimes illusory, whether the ideal man in *Wind, Sand, and Stars* who does what he wants and can escape dull routine is nonexistent. This note of pessimism is at variance with her customary feeling of optimism, her sense of her own power and self-direction.

HOW MUCH PERSONAL RELATION?

The autonomous girl makes it very clear that she, like other adolescent girls, has not yet experienced intimacy and love.

She talks about loving participation with members of her family but these are relationships that she had little part in creating. In her preadolescent days, her relations with girl friends were less ambivalent, less partial, and more complete than at present. Her relationships with boys indicate little loving participation. Participation in another's life implies "shared suffering" [6] and she is not ready for such suffering. She feels weighed down by the burdens of intimacy. "It gets so tense. You start worrying about someone else's problems. Your whole life becomes part of that person's life." "At first it's rosy. Then there are problems and you can't cope with them. You don't want to go through that again." "It's depressing after a while. There aren't too many people you can find that much interest in when there are so many interesting ones you haven't met yet." "I try not to date steady. I've been attached to one boy for six months. With the last boy it was about a year."

She usually necks and pets and may be aroused by the boy's closeness and attention and by the excitement that surrounds the dating game. But she gives little indication that she must exercise great restraint to keep from "going all the way" in her sexual relations. She associates having sexual intercourse with being in love and she has not yet experienced love. "I neck and pet with guys but I've never felt strongly enough about a boy to feel that I was his, to do with what he wants," one girl affirms. "You neck heavily in high school. But there's the fear of pregnancy and it's too complicated to get contraceptives. We're not that involved with boys," says another; and another, "Sex is natural. But you keep it pretty moderate." Another, "A girl goes all the way if she is really close."

Much time is required, she recognizes, for a love relationship to develop. She doesn't see her sexual feelings as maturing independently of a love relationship.

She seems to possess some of the requisites necessary for achieving intimacy and love. My impression comes from her talk and not from action indicating intimate, loving relations, since she is just beginning such action.

She has a feeling for what fidelity implies, a feeling for the

[6] Andras Angyal, *Neurosis and Treatment: A Holistic Theory*, E. Hanfmann and R. M. Jones (eds.) (New York: John Wiley & Sons, Inc., 1965), p. 24.

pleasure that derives from giving to others. "I saw relationships after reading *The Little Prince* that I never would have seen before," she explains. "The simple love that evolved between the proud flower and the little prince; the uniqueness of the flower for the little prince since he has nursed and cared for it; the responsibility felt by the little prince and the fox for each other because they tamed each other." [7]

She seems to have a deep sense of trust of other persons. "My mother couldn't understand that I trusted the boy to tell me about the bike that I wanted to buy from him, its merits and deficiencies. My mother says, 'You're being idealistic.' " She feels that she has retained the openness and innocence and trust of childhood and she may deplore the contrasting rigidities of adults. *"The Episode of the Sparrows* was so fabulous," she claims. "It shows how society destroys the innocence of young children. A little girl who wants a garden steals dirt from a rich woman and money from the church to buy seeds. Adults lose the capacity to see as the children do though some have kept their imagination and a viewpoint that's open. With more responsibilities and obligations, adults usually become more inhibited."

She gives some indication that though she has a sense of personal responsibility she can "let herself go" with abandon. The following statements could not have come from the adult-oriented girl.

I like the Beatles. The spirit of joy in living and doing things is wonderful. Their gay abandon, not working like fiends for some noble purpose, just having a good time. . . .

Sex is a personal thing. It affects two people but not anyone else.

Though many autonomous girls date frequently, some attractive and gregarious girls confide that they have rarely "gone with" boys. The explanations they give: their marginal position as upper-middle-

---

[7] Her words sound very much like Fromm's, "To love a person productively implies to care and to feel responsible for his life, not only for his physical existence but for the growth and development of all his human powers. To love productively is incompatible with being passive, with being an onlooker at the loved person's life; it implies labor and care and the responsibility for his growth." (Erich Fromm, *Man For Himself* [New York: Holt, Rinehart & Winston, Inc., 1947], pp. 100-101.)

class Negro, the tortures of being with a boy one doesn't like, the immaturity of the high school boy, his preference for going out in groups, his present involvement in studies or his not perceiving the girl romantically. "In college, boys feel more relaxed," a girl speculates. "They will like girls later on." With some girls there is the feeling, "I'm going to college and have plenty of time." For others, "I'm seventeen. I should have dated some by now." Generally, though, there is an absence of frenzy, whatever the dating pattern.

The girl, whether she dates or does not date, may have progressed farther in her intellectual, aesthetic, or political pursuits than in her personal relations with a boy. A girl doesn't always grow up evenly. Yet it is my premise that autonomous self-direction is a precondition for intimate relations with others in post-high school years.

The autonomous girl does not restrict her social relationships to any one class, religion, or racial group.[8] When she attends a school where girls segregate themselves by religion or race, she belongs to a nonsectarian or an interracial group, or else she intermingles. A Negro girl says, "I belong to two cultures: the intellectual and the Negro" (and she recognizes that she bears the scars and the advantages of such marginality). A white girl says, boastfully perhaps, "Any group in school is penetrable to me."

The high school girl, even among the autonomous, rarely speaks about the self-fulfillment that comes from rearing children. Such self-fulfilling activity is not generally within a high school girl's purview. Probably she must develop to a greater degree her own assertive, autonomous self before she develops the capacity to sur-

---

[8] The racially mixed couples dating in high school usually comprise a Negro boy and a white girl. Some of the autonomous girls, in trying to explain this pattern, indicate differing motivations of the girl and the boy. "White girls choose Negro boys, my mother says. I don't think so. The Negro boy is uplifting himself," one Negro girl asserts. "It's harder for a white boy than a white girl—the way boys stick together. A boy wouldn't want to break away that much. He would be ostracized," says a second Negro girl. "Some boys are friendly, though, and might enjoy a Negro girl's company. A lot of white girls are doing it for sheer rebellion," she adds. A white girl gives her opinion: "I think white boys are scared. Negro boys are very attractive, more so than Negro girls in our school. Their hulking manliness is absent from a great many of the white boys." A few Negro girls still in high school date older white boys.

render herself in this loving relationship of her own making. Perhaps as an adolescent she has not yet experienced in her relations with others the joy that comes from giving without expectation of return. One autonomous eighteen-year-old seems the exception. A talented art student, she wants to be an illustrator of children's books. She draws portraits of the children of her parents' friends. She would like to have many children, she says, and work in her home after marriage, "close to the family." Her remarks about the fulfillment to be derived from the rearing of children are authenticated by the quiet, capable manner with which she captivates the two-and-a-half-year-old who is present during the interview.

The autonomous high school girl generally seems not to bear out the assertion of Helene Deutsch that ". . . many women who preserve the activity of their egos, and use it for sublimation purposes, are extremely passive and masochistic in their sexual behavior. . . ." [9] On the contrary, she gives many indications that she will become as active and assertive in her sexual life as she has already become in other areas of her living, satisfying her own needs in addition to satisfying her lover.[10]

HER IDOLS

Her idols are often not early authority figures but rather young people with strong devotion to an honorable cause. "I feel kinship with a guy named Dick who is twenty-three. He's just a Negro guy working in the South who inspires me," explains

[9] Helene Deutsch, *The Psychology of Women*, I (New York: Grune & Stratton, Inc., 1944), 247.

[10] A woman who feels full equality with men and thus enlarges the area of shared experiences is richer sexually, Alice Rossi contends. In support of this thesis she points to Maslow's findings that the more "dominant" the woman, the greater her ability to give herself freely in love. She enjoys sexual fulfillment to a much greater degree than the conventionally feminine woman. *See* Alice S. Rossi, "Equality Between the Sexes: An Immodest Proposal," *Daedalus* (Spring 1964), p. 648; A. H. Maslow, "Dominance, Personality and Social Behavior in Women," *Journal of Social Psychology*, X (1939), 3-39, and "Self-Esteem (Dominance Feeling) and Sexuality in Women," *Journal of Social Psychology*, XVI (1942), 259-294; Betty Friedan, in *The Feminine Mystique* (New York: W. W. Norton & Company, Inc., 1963), pp. 316-328, reviews Maslow's studies.

one white girl. "He works feverishly, is young, smart, devoted, could be making plenty of money doing something else. He is 'charged' with it." And she adds, "Ellen K. is a mother, a perfectly charming lady who went down to Mississippi. It makes you think, 'that's the kind of person I want to be.'" Another girl says, "My idols are principally the students in the South. They are able to live by their values." The girl's hero, then, is generally the "ordinary" person, whether man or woman, who gives of herself without receiving the power, the adulation, or the financial return accorded the men at the top.

She admires those who are close to her in years and who are making of their lives what she aspires to. "My cousin is going to the Sorbonne. She can speak French. She is educated and intellectual. She can do everything she wants in her marriage. She is twenty."

Among public persons, the late President Kennedy holds a unique position as the embodiment of the prime virtues. Girl after girl speaks of him with worshipful affection. Besides youthfulness, vigor, and personal charm, he is seen as having possessed knowledge, courage, and dedication—a man "with ideals who put them into practice."

HER INVOLVEMENT IN THE
LARGER COMMUNITY

The autonomous girl often indicates that she wants to expand opportunities for the deprived. In such participation, at her best she is learning to experience the gratification that comes from giving to others and she is developing mastery and competence in an area of importance to her.

In the civil rights movement, she is seen most clearly in her practical commitment to contemporary battle. She is the activist, her pace is quick, and her mind, she feels, is "open." She is impatient with the haste of the bitter militant and the slowness of the eternal compromiser.

Of the bitter militant, she says: "If you can't talk, you get nowhere. Riots don't accomplish anything; they're usually only instances of mob hysteria.

You have to compromise sometimes. You can't be a complete purist. Everything's not going to come all of a sudden."

Of the eternal compromiser, she says: "I'm not so passive. I get terribly angry. Sometimes I'd have to scream. Sometimes people have to be shocked into knowing the truth."

She feels she does not now have to demonstrate her authenticity by martyrdom. "There's no reason to do anything here in the North to get thrown into jail," one activist says. "I've read the laws that apply and they make sense."

She looks for a place in the social structure where her services can be utilized. She works through various organizations to send food, clothing, and books where they are needed and she performs all of the accompanying tasks—ringing doorbells, typing, filing, unpacking, and repacking. She marches for peace and she pickets a "low quality" Negro school and a local barber shop which was discriminating against Negroes.[11] She tutors young children and works for voter registration.

She believes that a girl must be informed before she acts but is disdainful of those who "talk an awful lot but don't do a great deal."

She wants to find in the Peace Corps "some purpose in life, something to live for. You can really get a feeling you're doing something good for people and having them do something for themselves. You feel as though you have a role in the world's being."

The "hands off" attitude of the Beatnik, so much at variance with her own approach to the world, is condemned. "They're the saddest bunch of people I know. They say, 'We wash our hands of the mess you've given us.' I disagree with that. Every generation is handed problems. They give up, they're quitters." "Sometimes they try too hard—in scoffing and scorning anything that has to do with school or school spirit."

She has the courage to risk being an outsider. She isn't always

[11] One girl describes the picketing of the local barber shop that was violating state law by not serving Negroes. "We sent Negroes and whites to the barber shop simultaneously. The whites were served and the Negroes were told they had to have appointments. We went in and told them that what they were doing was wrong. We picketed the shop from 12:30 to 1:30. Since then, they've been serving Negroes."

the "good girl" who does what the authorities demand. She is undeterred by name-calling or stereotyping—for example, "Communist," "Beatnik," "do-gooder," "radical"—whether it comes from parents, teachers, or peers. "If you take part in direct action, you're considered queer. You can't get involved." What can they really do to her, she muses. For example, the teacher who calls her a "truant" and does not allow her to make up a test when she is ill shortly after being the spokesman for a group integrating a local barber shop "can't change my grades if I do well on tests."

She describes the evolution of her desire to help change the world. A white Protestant girl, she had been searching for ideals to which she could commit herself. When she caught a glimpse of a different world, she was prepared for the awakening.

I was working for voter registration in the fourth ward. Some of those homes were like the 1890's—ceilings coming down, so poor. Even the homes of kids from my class. And I think of our five bathrooms! It's another world.

For the longest time, I had nothing I really cared about. I read and read and I had no direction. I had no reason for working hard accomplishing anything. I needed something to channel my efforts. Now I know where I'm going. I always knew I'd do something with people. They can use me.

A Negro girl, though in important ways an advantaged person herself, recognizes her own marginality when she returns to public school from an equalitarian boarding school and she identifies her own plight with the disadvantaged group.

I went to a boarding school where most of the students were white. I'm aware of the opportunities Negroes are missing. I feel an obligation. I'm not a Negro's Negro. I don't feel an allegiance with my race. But I'm judged as are Negroes en masse.

I think my parents are satisfied where they are now. Most of their friends have good jobs. They have no contact with lower-class Negroes. They don't acknowledge their existence. I was at an idealistic age and became aware of the civil rights movement. I am more touched than my parents by the lost opportunities.

Not all autonomous high school girls display this kind of involvement in the larger community. My sample includes many girls who were active in the civil rights movement. I mention elsewhere my unsuccessful attempt to find autonomous girls seriously involved in the arts.

MARRIAGE AND CAREER

The autonomous girl is not limiting herself to any specific path to marriage and career. She is becoming increasingly aware of alternative paths and she wants the freedom to choose marriage and/or career when the time is ripe. She doesn't need to know as a teen-ager at what age she will marry or what the rest of her life is going to be like. She hasn't met enough people, she feels, nor has she had enough experience to know what she is looking for in a mate. "I'm not too much interested in early marriage. I haven't even been in love yet so I can't comprehend marriage." "If I decide to have a career and that winds up being the most important thing to me, that's what I'll do. If I fall in love and want both marriage and career, and he understands, then I'll get married. There's no chronological age for marriage. You marry when you're mature enough to know that you really love someone." "When I'm that age I'll probably know. Even more than love there has to be respect, when the glamour wears off. The girl who finds immediate marriage important may have stopped looking for things, or maybe she has found what she is looking for."

She begins to direct her thinking toward what she is looking for in college and career: an M.A., a Ph.D.? Social work, journalism, or speech therapy? Often she mentions four or five possibilities. What are my talents, what do I like, she asks herself? Or, how can I serve best? "I feel I have to give the world something. I wouldn't give up having children for singing but I'd like to combine them." "I'm not going to spend my life cleaning house. My life must have some purpose." "I want to be a social worker. I want to give something to people." What career is feasible with marriage and family, she may also ask. "I wouldn't work while the children are growing up. Working depends upon what my husband does, how it fits in."

The autonomous high school girl thus prepares for alternative ways of life rather than foreclosing her future in her hunt for a man. Her future encompasses, in her terms, the best of all possible worlds, including intimacy and love for a man as well as intellectual development. She seems to sense that the paths could be mutually enriching, her autonomous intellectual development adding to what she can give and receive in marriage.

BELIEF IN GOD

She often regards belief in God as a kind of dependence that is antithetical to her desire to depend on herself. She wants to feel that she determines the course of her own life and its meaning and so lives it that the world has been made richer by her presence. "People control their own destinies. You're not controlled by Someone up there. You have to depend upon yourself, have faith in yourself."

She remains noncommittal about her belief in God. "Sometimes I do believe, sometimes I don't." "I'm not really definite in my opinion about God or religion." "I really haven't studied it enough to say anything." "I see intelligent people who believe so deeply —there must be something." "I can make no decision about religion until I know more about myself."

She questions whether religion can serve for her the function of comprehensibility or solace.[12] "I'd like to believe there's Something up there but I don't." "What if I were born of a different faith?" "Doesn't it strain the boundaries of credulity to believe in a God who 'pulls strings?' " "Is there something really like heaven? Doesn't your soul die when you die?"

That she feels she doesn't have the final answer yet about religion is indicated by her desire to learn more. She wants to take special courses. Or she hopes to read on her own about the different religions. One autonomous girl is ready to "start again" with religion.

[12] A girl who hasn't seen her father for many years looks to God for solace. "I have a child's idea of the Almighty Father," she says. "It's very reassuring at times. You can tell your problems to Him. He will understand if no one else will."

"I understand the comfort to be found in a faith," another autonomous girl asserts. "I've found this comfort in my family. Maybe if that weren't enough, I'd turn to religion."

"I used to be agnostic. Religion is something to cling to, I thought. I do want my children to go to church, to have a moral background, a feeling for God. It's something to believe in when you're weak or need something."

Most of the autonomous girls who were interviewed come from homes where parents were college-educated. Many come from minority racial and religious groups. Educational and social opportunities for both parents and children seem a necessary (though not a sufficient) condition for the development of autonomy in children, at least as evidenced by high school girls.

Is the autonomous girl mentally healthy? According to Erich Fromm, "Mental health, in the humanistic sense, is characterized by the ability to love and to create, by the emergence from the incestuous ties to family and nature, by a sense of identity based on one's experience of self as the subject and agent of one's powers, by the grasp of reality inside and outside of ourselves, that is, by the development of objectivity and reason." "Free man is by necessity insecure; thinking man by necessity uncertain." [13] In these terms, the autonomous girl that we have described, more than any other, is mentally healthy.

[13] Erich Fromm, *The Sane Society* (New York: Holt, Rinehart & Winston, Inc., 1955), pp. 203, 196. The autonomous girl resembles Fromm's productively oriented person who develops her active powers to such an extent that she is not submerged in her world but related to it (*Ibid.*, p. 197).

nine

OTHER PATTERNS
SEEN AT THE
MENTAL HOSPITAL

HOSPITALIZATION: LACK OF AUTONOMY
AND WITHDRAWAL FROM RELATION

Hospitalization may prolong a girl's dependence upon others and help to sustain her lack of autonomy, the girl assuming that the regression privileges of a patient are hers for keeps. This dilemma of hospitalization is recognized by the staff. Usually a girl remains for a maximum of one year at the private hospital and for an even shorter period at one of the state hospitals.[1]

Though the girl views her "illness" as something she should control, she nonetheless is aware of advantages in the patient role. Her sickness gives her an excuse and justification for unseemly conduct and divests her of personal responsibility. One girl abusively asks an attendant whether she drinks, smokes opium, or takes dope, and justifies such wayward questions by, "I'm sick." Another attaches a name to her deviance: she asserts that she is "paranoid," always suspicious of people. Sickness exempts a girl from customary social performance. She tells the group worker not to "appoint" girls to committees, they must "volunteer." She tells the dance instructor not to have contests. "It won't work with us. We have enough problems. We shouldn't compete."

The girl regards herself as sick throughout her stay, though she

---

[1] A brief description of hospital life is given in the Appendix.

perceives a change in the severity of her illness. During the initial period she is optimistic: this is a vacation and she will stay the minimum period of two months, then leave and rejoin her classmates. This optimism helps to numb the shock of hospitalization. She has not yet acknowledged that she is a hospital patient, removed from the community.

The minimum period passes and she doesn't leave. She becomes despondent, feels she is getting worse. She may plan to run away and explains in justification: "A girl must regress before she can progress." She begins to "lose control" of herself and is no longer her own agent. But evidence of regressive behavior in a peer may engender anxiety. To maintain some autonomy is still her goal and regression indicates a lack of autonomy. The girls stare mutely as Bonny, who has been a patient for eighteen months and, according to group consensus, has improved considerably, once again goes through her contortions. They assemble elsewhere and talk about epileptics they have seen in other hospitals, about the "fit" a girl's mother once had, about a girl's own tantrums when she thinks of her problems and shakes her leg nervously. Bonny bothers her, one girl explains, because she sees herself, her own mannerisms, in Bonny.

Eventually the girl feels that she is getting better and talks about future plans outside the hospital. She is ready to relinquish the patient role. She doesn't do the crazy things she used to, now she "acts out" by climbing trees instead of in more destructive ways, one girl boasts. Now she thinks what is troubling her before getting excited and often she doesn't get excited as a result, says another. Her parents have been helped, too. They used to say, "Buck up." They didn't understand that she couldn't. And a third claims that her ups and downs are not so extreme as they used to be; she is getting well.

The time for departure approaches and the girl, panicky and fearful, sees herself as still sick. If the doctors knew some of the things about her that she hasn't told, she probably wouldn't be going home. Does the doctor really understand her problems, she wonders.

Though the girl is fearful when she makes her departure, one ear is always attuned to the outside during her stay. She is at present "out of tune" in her relations at home or school but that is where she belongs. The sanctuary that the hospital provides has less appeal than the demands outside. She eagerly awaits letters and expresses disappointment when she gets none. There is pandemonium the day the news leaks out that weekend leave will be limited to one day instead of two. Much as she may wallow in its protectiveness, she accepts the role of patient only tentatively and circumspectly; she is self-conscious and sensitive in the role. She doesn't want to be known as "a hospital girl" on the trips she takes. She asks why books aren't written to explain the "inner problems" of people who go to mental hospitals so that little children won't say, "They're 'bats' in there." She wants to know why people think that a mental hospital is for the insane; nobody could tell anything was wrong with her until they got to know her very well. She wants to know what a departing girl is going to say to her classmates when she returns to school.

What goes wrong in her relations with others, the girl at the private hospital asks, and she answers in the language of psychotherapy. She describes her mechanisms of defense in her early encounters with hospital authorities: "Six attendants had to get me from the TV room. They call it *regressive* activity. I'm glad they have a name for it. Biting your nails and smoking and acting like a baby." She tries to pinpoint her defense mechanisms in analyzing her relationship with her chum: "I know what's wrong. I *identify* with you and pretty soon I'll be *projecting* on to you and that's bad for me." "And for me, too," concurs the chum. In such vein, the private hospital girl demonstrates her verbal facility as well as the hospital's orientation around analytic psychotherapy.

The state hospital girl is less sophisticated than the private hospital girl about concepts of emotional illness. In contrast to the private hospital girl, she has been "put away" and she is told that she is "sick." Consequently she bandies the word about, referring usually to her peers and occasionally to herself, but what "sick" means is not clear to her. "I am disturbed—that means 'nervous' —but I'm calmer now," says one girl. "My mother doesn't think there is anything wrong with you. I told her you are boy-crazy," says another. They tell how they cover their faces with their hands when club women come to visit, say silly things, and make silly requests. "These girls are very sick," they hear a club woman say. A girl who "goes into one of her fits" they see as "sick," explaining that she gets depressed and can't help herself. Hearing "voices" or displaying such infantile behavior as whining and scratching are also seen as "mental" or "sick." A "sick" girl is generally tolerated by her peers if they do not identify or compete with her or find her a nuisance. When one of the girls has an acute psychotic attack and walks around unkempt and semi-dressed, mumbling to herself, a girl who laughs is sharply admonished by the other girls.

The girl at the state hospital is likely to see herself as "bad" rather than "sick." She is often the Delinquent described in Chapter Six. She has been bad, has been "put away," is serving her time, and her prime goal is to leave the hospital. Being "bad" is less traumatic than being "sick." If a girl is "bad," she doesn't act "social," according to the prescribed norms. In contrast, if a girl is "sick," she doesn't act "human," she doesn't have "her wits about her."

Am I good or bad, asks an overgrown Negro girl, born out of wedlock and placed in foster homes and institutions for most of her thirteen years. Is there something wrong with her? she wants to know. When she does things that are bad, she thinks she hears God telling her to be good. She shows me her Bible open to the passage that her calendar tells her is the verse for the day. She interprets the passage, and then continues: what is wrong with her? Why does she hear God? She wants to understand herself but she can't.

Such obsessions with good and bad seem to weigh heavily on the Catholic Puerto Rican girls. To the charge nurse, they appear guilt-ridden and anxious to expiate their guilt through good works. One Puerto Rican girl spends much of the morning washing, mopping, and cleaning the porch over and over again. Another, too, often cleans and recleans. And a third paces up and down the hall hearing voices, "the good and the bad."

The judgment of the state hospital girl that "sickness" has greater stigma than "badness" is often reinforced by the attendants. "Most of these girls are not mental cases, they're not sick, they're just bad," says one attendant. "I think the girls who aren't sick shouldn't be hospitalized, they shouldn't have this stigma. There should be some cottages for them off the hospital grounds."

OTHER PATTERNS OF DEVIANCE

Delinquents and anarchic bohemians were found inside the hospital as well as in the community. Other patterns of deviance that were observed inside the hospital include:

1. The adult-oriented girl in caricature
2. The infantile disrupter: the teen-ager who acts the child
3. The little old lady who gives up the struggle to live among her peers
4. The mute schizophrenic: the girl who forfeits her language
5. The mobile girl with insoluble dilemmas.

Each of these patterns is described briefly below.

THE ADULT-ORIENTED GIRL
IN CARICATURE

The adult-oriented girl in caricature—Beth, for example, at the private hospital—sees her mother as all-knowing and responds to her demands with complete submission. She is the good daughter who obeys and worships her mother. Her mother knows best and can do everything best. The higher her mother rises in her daughter's estimation, the lower she, the daughter, falls.[2] Her father she sees through her mother's eyes as somewhat contemptible. The black-or-white family relationship carries over to her perception of staff. She speaks admiringly of the chief psychiatrist as "the head who really knows her work," but she is contemptuous of the "lowly" attendants. She relates to adults not as persons but according to their position in the hierarchical structure.

Beth, dubbed the "preacher" by her peers, is a self-righteous

---

[2] The more autonomous girl is free to see her mother as a whole person, to accept the good and reject the bad. She is not operating on the "all or none" principle but experiences the nuances and contradictions that make up her mother as a human being.

girl who is aloof in words and manner and doesn't speak or understand the peer language. She sits by herself, her head high in the air,
very stern and very stiff. When she talks, she often pontificates.
The girls never want to talk to her, she complains. She is sometimes
outspokenly critical of them, asking to be given a sedative because
her roommates keep her awake, laughing at one girl's "spindly" legs
and another's "fat face." She lacks levity and takes seriously what
her peers say in jest or as a lark or a diversion.

Though she would like to be an "ordinary" adolescent, at
eighteen she has given up the struggle. Maybe some girls can skip
adolescence, she says, they don't have to spend years thinking about
unessential things. Most of her life has been spent with adults.

Her attitude toward her body indicates rigidity and rejection
rather than a sense of pleasure. When she paints a mural that is
a copy of Lautrec, she refuses to show the breasts, as Lautrec does,
in order not to have any "sex" in the picture. Though a student of
the arts, she is repelled by the nudes that she sees in the art books—
even those of Renoir and Titian. Her dress for the fashion show she
considers too tight, despite the girls' denial. "I don't want to show
my lines," she insists as she slips on a cardigan.

Now eighteen, she expresses the anguish of first experience with
a boy when she meets her first boy friend at the hospital. There is
the problem: what to do with him, what to say to him. She is
meeting him at the square dance and she wonders whether she
should go over and say, "Hi."

The love fantasy with her therapist is recounted to all who will
listen. "I love him," she affirms. "I think I'll write him a letter and
tell him so. He's my first. I don't think I should beat around the
bush." Her peers are disdainful of this unreciprocated fervor: "It
shouldn't bother us if she wants to make a fool of herself. She has
to learn the hard way." Beth doesn't seek intimacy or love in a
relation. She asks for little because, despite her haughtiness, she
feels that she has little to offer.

She sees herself as a dedicated artist. "Everybody is trying to
marry me off, and I'm not going to marry," she insists. "There are
too many other things—art, dance, sociology—and you're not free
when you marry." She has already achieved some competence in

several of the arts but her artistic products reproduce her essential motif. The sculpture she makes is like a piece from a Victorian boudoir. The medieval servant that she paints resembles the Joan of Arc she identifies with. Her interest in the arts (and also in religion) may well be in inverse relationship to her social competence.

Her intellectual or artistic ventures are limited by her poverty in autonomy and relation. The true artist is deeply related to other persons and to the community. Rooted in these commitments, he is able to withdraw temporarily from relation, to get beyond himself and envisage a new world. Beth, though, can't transcend her self because she has little self. She is committed in relation only to her mother, and she is unable to withdraw from this relation.

Nobility and a great destiny are her lot, she fantasies. If she can't be important in reality, she, or those close to her, can be all-important in fantasy. She often thinks about a girl she knows who dreamed about visits from Christ. A very remarkable girl! Only her (Beth's) mother had a facial expression like that girl's.

In contrast to her glorification of self, she also negates self. She says that she feels as though she is not Beth, but somebody else inhabiting her body. Her soul, or part of it, is gone. She can't write any more, she has great difficulty even composing letters. Thus, she is not only the Great one but also No one. The exclusive relationship with her mother has left no room for growth.

THE INFANTILE DISRUPTER: THE
TEEN-AGER WHO ACTS THE CHILD

Molly is younger and smaller than most of the girls at the private hospital. Her relations with peers during her first day at the hospital are a prelude of what is to come. She talks to the girls about baseball. Does she know any boys in her community? they ask. Only her father, she responds. The girls exchange knowing glances. She joins the girls at Scrabble but leaves the game abruptly, taking her pen with her. She doesn't want the girls using her ball-point pen, she asserts. She joins the ping-pong game but plays very poorly and subsequently complains that the girls won't play with her. She wants to be served her food first to be sure that she gets everything. Frustrated, she whines and pushes and kicks. She flies a kite in her room, to the apparent consternation and amusement of the girls. A girl asks her condescendingly if she can do the nine-table, and she obliges. "It will take a long time, but Molly will grow up," one group member predicts.

Molly did not start to grow up or to be accepted by the group during her three months at the private hospital. She remains a constant irritant to the girls. Although a few girls are protective of her, the group never sees her as another adolescent. Sue appears to express the consensus of the group when she says, "She isn't one of us. What would she talk about if she were here? She'd probably take out her Annie Oakley gun and start shooting."

Molly is seen a year later at the state hospital, and she now frequently runs from her peer group, which frightens her, to realms where she can excel: as a Jew steeped in orthodoxy and as a student steeped in mathematics. She notifies me of Jewish services. Weeks ahead, she asks if I know the time of sunset on the eve of the Jewish New Year. She wishes to make me a Jewish calendar. She appears to want to identify with me, an adult, against her peers. Moreover, her withdrawal into her books further isolates her from peers. She often has a textbook on the ward, which her mother has brought from home.

Molly has acquired a chum, her first close peer relationship. Between her one friend, her books, and her religion, she establishes a *modus vivendi*. Her tentative moves toward the group often encounter rejection but with her new experience in relation she is not so easily rebuffed. She still has little, though, to offer her peers. She doesn't dance, wears her dresses too long, doesn't go with boys, doesn't usually "put herself out" for other girls, and her whining probably reminds the girls of younger siblings they left behind.

Molly begins to develop a new image of her body. "I mustn't eat so much or my hips will get too large," she says. This hardly seems the girl who saw herself as Annie Oakley a year earlier. And, though at her first hospital dance she feels that she must "save herself" for her (nonexistent) boy friend at home, she later begins to dance and talk with boys.

Her backsliding is evident during her menstrual period when she reemploys the early childhood weapons of whining and stamping.

"My mother, that's my trouble," Molly explains. She "fights" her dominating mother in her fantasies. She sees a boy who practices the violin (on the Thematic Apperception Test) as "thinking up a way to deceive his mother about violin practice so he can go out and play baseball. In the end, though, he'll play the violin." She sees a little girl "more interested in playing with dolls than learning her schoolwork. The mother, determined to teach, is angry at the daughter because of her lack of interest."

She "fights" her dominating mother through her "epileptic seizures" ("Those were childish temper tantrums and not epileptic fits," the charge nurse tells her) and through her whining and eating difficulties—that is, through being the infantile disrupter and remaining the child.

She indicates fearfulness (on the Thematic Apperception Test) about the relationship between man and woman. In her statements she may be giving us a synopsis of her own life.

I don't know. A woman? A man? You don't think she's killing him, do you?

A man strangles his wife in her sleep. He's sorry now. He pleads temporary insanity and goes to a hospital for the criminally insane.

A man is coming in late, through the window. He is probably two-timing his wife and doesn't want her to know. He's too handsome for a burglar. He's possibly a juvenile delinquent.

We may conjecture that she sees the encounter between her parents as a battle, and her mother appears to be killing any self-assertion on her father's part. In a fit of anger her father "strangles" his wife; he convinces himself he can live without her. But he is really a nice guy, given a decent chance. "Stop me from doing this," he says. "Be a wife and not a tyrant." He is the little boy misbehaving, a juvenile delinquent, who shamefacedly comes home to mother.

Molly may be saying, in dream-like fashion, that "he" is really "she" herself, since her mother gives her the same treatment she gives her father. Mother tries to make her into a premature adult, disallowing play and allowing only serious adult study. Is my mother killing me? she asks. Molly strangles her mother, who has "strangled" her autonomous growth, and is then sent to the mental hospital. In the final scene, she is two-timing her mother, rebelling against her.

THE LITTLE OLD LADY
WHO GIVES UP THE STRUGGLE
TO LIVE AMONG HER PEERS

The childlike girl with a look of resigned serenity reminiscent of a little old lady has been in the state hospital for about five years, since she was twelve. She has never had a chum and does not know the name of the girl who regularly sits across from her at mealtime. She rocks back and forth in her rocking chair on the adolescent ward, her fingers in her mouth. She plays with two kittens, then watches television. Surrounded by girls who express an avid interest in clothes, she never changes her wardrobe.

Occasionally she seems to share the world of her peers. One evening she dances with another girl, and the attendant on duty is called in to watch. "Look," the girls exclaim. "Grace is dancing!" Grace wears a new dress and says pridefully, "It's too long. But I'll grow into it."

Grace rarely has visitors. An aunt who does come one day spends much of her time on the hospital grounds cleaning out her station wagon. Finally she appears on the ward with some cut-outs, fruit, and candy, then leaves early. Grace seems ecstatic during and after the visit.

A few weeks later, after Grace is transferred to an adult ward, "with the old ladies," she continues to clutch a torn paper bag with one lollipop—the last remains from her aunt's visit. Does she miss anybody from the adolescent ward? I ask her. "Yes, the cats." Could I bring one over for her to see? She likes it better here, she says, and the adults like her, an attendant informs me.

The girls say that Grace will have to stay in the hospital for two more years. "What did she do?" is the query. "She didn't do anything, but she doesn't have any place to go," is the response.

Grace would concur. "No one wants me home—ever," she says with terseness and finality. Her mother has been hospitalized since Grace was an infant, and Grace has been doled out from relative to institution to relative. She has learned to take care of her simple needs and to help others in simple tasks. All the while she seems to remain unruffled.

Whereas the problems of the adult-oriented girl in caricature and the infantile disrupter revolve primarily around autonomy, the problems of the little old lady revolve primarily around relation. She has been abandoned. Her experiences in relations of companionship and intimacy have apparently been so minimal that, unlike the delinquent, she has given up the search for relation.

THE MUTE SCHIZOPHRENIC: THE GIRL WHO FORFEITS HER LANGUAGE

When Isabel first appears on the ward, she clutches tightly the nurse's hand and seems to be crying. The girls stare at her. Pointing to the nurse's purse, she indicates her desire for ice cream. The nurse departs with her to get some. After the nurse leaves for the day, the girls exclaim, one after another, "Stop that, Isabel." "Isabel just scratched me." "She's hitting everybody."

Isabel is usually mute. Though her face may be expressive, she says nothing. She seems to understand everything I say as I walk and talk with her but usually her eyes are elsewhere: on the doll for a minute, on the kittens, on the pumpkin decorations, though not sustained anywhere. She hears music in the next ward. "I want to go to the music," she whispers in my ear. She goes in to dinner with me and holds my hand firmly during dinner and during the several hours I spend with her.

One girl appears to see aspects of herself in Isabel. "She gives me the creeps. My eyes used to pop out like hers," she confesses. Another seems to derive some perverse pleasure from holding Isabel's hand, then running away and laughingly repeating my primitive conversation with Isabel. "If she continues to cry like that, I won't be able to sleep, I can't take that," says a third girl.

Isabel has never had a relationship of attachment or affection either with her peers or with adults. It is only the inanimate that now claims her involvement: a radio, a paint set. Otherwise she is either seclusive or assaultive.

In her family Isabel evidently experienced both hostility and abandonment. She was confirmed as the fearful, whining child of a vindictive mother and a reserved, absentee father. Deposited at the hospital at a tender age, she was rarely visited by her family in the dozen succeeding years though she occasionally received from them expensive gifts.

Isabel's relations with others have been so devastating that she can't even remain the contented cow, as does the little old lady. She must take the final leap into being a nonperson by foregoing that which defines humanity; the ability to communicate with others through language.

THE MOBILE GIRL WITH INSOLUBLE DILEMMAS

I define a mobile girl, in my conceptual framework, as one who tries to affirm herself in a manner in which she has not been confirmed. The mobile girl who finds her dilemmas insoluble —the girl who gets to the hospital—both rebels against and holds on to much that she is, and she both desires and fears to become something else. She illustrates most poignantly what Rank has called the fear of life (or "the anxiety of freedom") and the fear of death (the fear of being submerged in the whole, remaining encased in her ascribed group). She is the girl who seems most frantic about who she is and where she is going. Who am I? she asks aloud. Girl or boy? Lesbian or normal? Where do I belong? In the lower or upper class? Among Negroes or West Indians or whites? With the unthinking mass or the thinking elite?

Conflict over body and sexual performance

This girl is often worried about her body. Do I look like a girl? Can I perform the functions of a woman?

Sue, appraising her athletic-looking figure, her short, kinky hair, and her throaty voice, concludes that her mother must have had sex with a cow since she, Sue, looks like a cow. (She seems to be referring to the ungainly and ruminative qualities of the cow.) A few days later she displays a stuffed lamb and asserts that the girls now say she looks like a lamb. "I don't want to look like an animal," she declares. Presumably what she really doesn't want to look like is a boy. Her mother confirmed her as the boy—the tomboy—that she, the mother, wanted, and Sue wants to affirm herself as a girl. A new glow appears on her face the day the girls help her dress in more feminine fashion and apply make-up for the first time.

The mobile girl may camouflage her concern about her body and sexual performance through "horsing around"; for example, chasing, hitting, or rubbing food over another girl. Her provocation is half-serious, half in jest, and along with the seeming camaraderie are homosexual overtones. She seems to be going toward other girls and away from them simultaneously, possibly trying to make the final break and turn to a boy.

She is often preoccupied with the man's assumed need for sexual intercourse. She tells stories about men who made holes in mattresses to put their penises in, they were so frustrated. Man is insistent and pressuring, she feels, but woman, and specifically she, herself, is fearful.

The dilemma of class

The mobile girl in the hospital who expresses dissatisfaction and anxiety concerning her body and sexual functioning often experiences dissatisfaction with her social class, which is likely to be lower-middle.[3]

The daughter of a "blue-collar" worker, she often aspires to

---

[3] Though the girl who experiences dissatisfaction with her body need not be the same one who expresses dissatisfaction with her social status, she often is the same.

Kinsey found that the girl (or the boy) who rises from a lower level home into an upper educational level is likely to be more restrained sexually than the girl who originates in an upper level and stays there (Alfred C. Kinsey et al., *Sexual Behavior in the Human Female* [Philadelphia: W. B. Saunders Co., 1953], p. 297).

rise several steps on the social ladder and is preoccupied with her ascent when she comes to the middle-class surroundings of the private hospital. Perhaps it is in part her class aspiration that makes her a successful candidate for admission to this hospital. "How can I rise in social class?" "How should a girl socialize?" "What opportunities are there for money and fame? For 'cultured living'?" These are her questions and she finds herself insufficiently prepared for upward mobility.

Sue, a tomboyish girl from an economically marginal Jewish household, bemoans her difficulties in socializing and verbalizing. She was compelled to attend the girls' fashion show, she says, though she had nothing to wear and couldn't socialize or talk right, always had to use curse words. She reveals the importance she attributes to material display when she declares that she is unimpressed by the director who earns so much money, more than anybody else, and dresses as though he were a poor man.

Laura, a petite, attractive West Indian girl, chafes under her background of absentee father, washerwoman mother, and prostitute sisters. When the girls tell fortunes with cards, Laura wants to know if she is going to be rich, so rich that her husband won't have to work. Will she be pretty, cultured, intelligent? She jests about buying a mink jacket with earnings from her part-time hospital job. "I want to wear it every day. It's nothing at all," she shrugs.

The girl whose conflict revolves around her class shows disrespect and sometimes loathing for the hospital attendants who, she knows, are at the lowest rung of the achievement ladder.

Joan speaks disparagingly to the attendant, "You think you're high but you're not, you wouldn't know how to be, you're really very low."

Sue is abusive to the attendants, asks them whether they drink, smoke opium, take dope. She calls one attendant a prostitute, whereupon the attendant starts to cry, says she is quitting, and puts on her coat. Other girls implore her to stay.

The attendants are told that they lack ability, show little concern for the girls, and display uncertain emotional health. A girl may also use abusive language to a psychiatrist in authority but in self-punishment later bites her wrist until blood flows.

The dilemma associated with color

The mobile girl whose conflict is linked to color reacts
sensitively and passionately to her inferior color status. Her color
preoccupations invade almost every aspect of her living and her
accusations are often paranoid in flavor. She expresses self-hatred
for being Negro and hatred of others for their condemnation.

"If you don't like Negroes, why did you come here?" Adele asks Molly
accusingly. Adele is a dark, attractive Negro girl. She turns from the
innocent Molly to the magazine on her lap and mutters, "The bitches, they
don't want the Negroes to move in." Adele has been reading about a
Negro family who bought a home in a white neighborhood with disastrous
consequences and Molly is the innocent victim of her rage.

Early in my stay on the ward Adele's anger and resentment are focused
on me. She approaches me with the question, "Nurse, did you make your
dress?" "I have a name, I'm not a nurse," I respond. Whereupon Adele
becomes indignant. "What's the matter, are you ashamed of being a nurse?"
I can feel the anger well up in her. I try to appease her, to apologize, but
she turns away when I approach. Later that evening she calls me a "fucking instigator," and drones over and over a ditty about a "white man
stepping on a black man's toes." She is generally more pleasant the next
day but something still rankles within her. "The squares are sitting over
there," she says, and points in my direction.

Later in my stay, Adele confesses she didn't like me when I came, she
thought I was prejudiced. I seemed to snap, to be sharp when colored girls
came around.

Adele combines her display of defiance with an attempt to learn
Spanish in order to "pass" as a West Indian and thereby partially rectify
her derogatory definition of herself. She also tries to identify with a person
of higher color status. "I could go for you," she tells me. She makes it clear
that "going for" me means wanting to have what I have, what she assumes
comes with education in the middle-class white community.

A dilemma of values

An occasional mobile girl is embroiled in a dilemma
of values. Should she squander her days on the phone, in the beauty
parlor, at the dress shop, and at the afternoon social as her mother
has done, or is the world of the intellect and the arts open to her?

How does she affirm herself in such a manner when she has been confirmed by family and later by peers only in certain of her external characteristics—for example, as friendly or pretty?

Why can't the mobile girl affirm herself as she wishes and move on to where she wants to go?

She has to cope with (and probably accepts) society's verdict about the badness or lowliness of her heritage. She is nonwhite when it is "good" to be white, a Jew when it is "good" to be a non-Jew, a lower-class slum resident when it is "good" to be middle class.

But many girls are in the same boat. What makes her different from those peers who start with similar social handicaps and do move without apparent emotional mishap?

This girl feels alone, without any support. She can't depend on any relation. Within her family she has experienced a kind of "double bind." [4] Her mother has espoused freedom and individuation while clutching her tightly in a subtle and devastating fashion; she was manifestly neglectful or permissive but exerted covert pressures such as the induction of guilt. My mother is basically good but weak or the victim of social circumstances, the girl pines, and so am I betraying her by aspiring upward?

Outside her family, the mobile girl was encouraged to assume new roles and acquire new experiences either by those inexperienced themselves or by others whom she was unable to accept as models. These latter offered bait but never followed through in any convincing fashion. Will she be brought up merely to be thrown back again? she fearfully asks herself.

She requires of herself a superadequate performance in order to compensate for her unworthy past. Because of her lack of training and exposure at the level to which she aspires, she sets goals which are beyond her grasp. She is the lower-class girl who wants to be "cultured," a "lady."

---

[4] The mother here is expressing two orders of messages and one of them denies the other. *See* John H. Weakland, "The 'Double-Bind' Hypothesis of Schizophrenia and Three-Party Interaction," in Don D. Jackson, *The Etiology of Schizophrenia* (New York: Basic Books, Inc., Publishers, 1960), pp. 373-388.

In her seemingly insoluble dilemmas, she may lose herself temporarily in such a fence-sitting role as the clown. In this role she is not committing herself. The clown needs to be funny but displays a natural, spontaneous wit. Her caricaturing of people and animals and her interplay with her peers reveal a sardonic view of life. Her words and gestures amuse and animate the group. If a girl doesn't really know whether or not she can fit among her desired peers, she can play it safe in this role. She gets attention through her antics and indirectly expresses feelings that she is afraid to reveal more directly. She fears, moreover, that if she stops joking she won't have anything to talk about, that she will withdraw from people and feel lonely.[5]

She may act "as if" she were genuinely the sophisticate, poised and gracious, with measured traces of an upper-class accent, a pygmalion whose ancestry hardly shows. She may act "as if" she could continue indefinitely to be the leader and confidante who bears the burdens of her peers.

She may run away or try suicidal gestures to give fair warning of the tempest within her. And if no one "hears" her, as is their wont, she may resort to psychosis or suicide.

She desires the approval of her esteemed peers, often seemingly to an excessive degree. Sue can't understand herself, being so sensitive, wanting everybody to like her. Is she the same girl, she wonders, who saw her mother faint and stood coldly by? Out of her uncertainty about being confirmed as she wants to affirm herself, she may stack the cards against herself, "malevolently transforming" the situation by insulting and disparaging her peers (and adults),

---

[5] Pearson says of the clown role: "He may attempt to make the best of a bad job by accepting the fact that he is clumsy and awkward and parading it in accentuating fashion before others in order to obtain the pleasure of their laughter" (Gerald H. J. Pearson, *Adolescence and the Conflict of Generations* [New York: W. W. Norton & Company, Inc., 1958], p. 29).

Margaret Brenman sees the role of the clown as the masochist's way of maintaining an equilibrium. By the witty unmasking of others while caricaturing herself, she can express and yet hold within limits her aggressiveness ("On Teasing and Being Teased: And the Problem of 'Moral Masochism,'" in Ruth S. Eissler *et al.* (eds.), *The Psychoanalytic Study of the Child*, VII [New York: International Universities Press, 1952], 274).

especially if the encounter is new and therefore precarious.[6] Her disparaging statements may be followed by a quiet, "I like you."

Her inability to move forward or go back is evidenced in her intellectual pursuits. She busily memorizes the title, the painter, and the description of each painting in her new art book; or she listens to records, a book on the French impressionists in her hand. But she has difficulty in concentration and in persistent application. She derogates her actual performance. Sue, for example, whose natural talent for caricature far exceeds the second-rate caricaturist whom she copies, gives the explanation, "I can't do anything." Laura, a girl of superior endowment who yearns for at least high school graduation and business school, underrates her own intelligence.

The mobile girl, with her seemingly insoluble dilemmas concerning body and sexual performance, social status, and sometimes intellectual performance, can probably be characterized in Erikson's terms as being in a state of acute identity diffusion. Erikson speaks about the adolescent manifesting this state when she feels compelled to make crucial decisions and fears both making and not making these decisions. Some of the manifestations of identity diffusion: she can't concentrate, she can't compete, she becomes estranged from her national and ethnic origins, she adopts a negative identity.[7] All of these indications of identity diffusion appear among the mobile girls at the hospital.

She can also be characterized as a girl living in limbo, a state that prevents both autonomy and personal relation. She can't relate to others with fidelity since she is not sure who she is and where she belongs. She brings little genuine autonomy to personal relation.

Nor can she temporarily withdraw from relation and gain competence through serious involvement in areas of interest to her.

---

[6] Harry Stack Sullivan, in introducing the concept of "malevolent transformation," says that the child who discovers that his expression of the need for tenderness from his family inevitably brings anxiety or pain henceforth adopts the "basic malevolent attitude" that he lives among enemies (*The Interpersonal Theory of Psychiatry* [New York: W. W. Norton & Company, Inc., 1953], pp. 213-216).

[7] Erik H. Erikson, "The Problem of Ego Identity," in *Identity and the Life Cycle* (New York: International Universities Press, 1959), pp. 122-132.

Since she has no genuine relation, she is frantically concerned with relation and thus is handicapped in her autonomous pursuits. She brings little of personal relation to her autonomous efforts.

In summary, the girl who enters the mental hospital has been declared deviant. She may be a girl who pushes adult-orientation to its limit. She may be delinquent or anarchic bohemian. She may affirm herself as a nothing, as, for instance, the mute schizophrenic. She may remain in limbo, refusing to affirm herself as she has been confirmed and unable to affirm herself otherwise.

ten

A
CONCLUDING
NOTE

I should like to summarize the work and consider a few of its implications.

This is a study of the high school girl in the process of becoming a woman, of the major paths she follows as a conformist or else as deviant or autonomous. The autonomous girl has been taken as a model.

The autonomous girl engages in the autonomous process and in the beginnings of personal relation. As part of the autonomous process, she may pursue her own ideas to their limits. Such pursuit is reflected in the freshness and perceptiveness of her observations. She may engage in play, "letting herself go," the activity becoming and end in itself; or in work, for example, as a future scientist observing the world in the abstract or as a potential artist creating her own world. In all of this she develops the "I" of autonomy, a sense of difference and distinctness from others—*I* think, *I* feel, *I* know. She feels power in being the source of her own thoughts and feelings and the agent of her own actions.

The autonomous girl brings this power of self-agency to bear in her relations with others. She does not remain only the detached observer and is not engaged only in reciprocal role relations, but begins to give and receive affection and love in her relations with companions of her own choosing, with no strings attached.

We can look at the autonomous girl in the light of implications for morality, for mental health and pathology, and for societal goals.

In terms of morality: the autonomous girl, to live fully as a person, lives by the golden rule. Her autonomy is ultimately in the service of personal relation. She becomes a person not in autonomous pursuits but only in her relations of mutuality, intimacy, and love with other persons. If she were to destroy others or treat others as nonpersons, she could not interact with them as free agents, and the means by which she becomes a person would be destroyed. The destruction of others is a destruction of her self. Stereotyping of others may be efficient and perhaps necessary at times but morally the only justification of any such impersonal interaction is that it potentially be in the service of personal relation. It is in this context of autonomy's being in the service of relation that I find significant the fact that the civil rights movement has been so much a youth movement; and, more specifically, that Miss America 1966 aspires to medical school, pediatrics, and volunteer work in southeast Asia.

Looking at the autonomous girl from the standpoint of mental health and pathology, it has been my thesis that only the autonomous girl is mentally healthy. She is involved both in autonomous pursuits and in personal relations, and each enriches the other. During high school, her autonomous pursuits have outpaced her exclusive relations of intimacy and love, but she seems to be developing the requisites for such relations. She has been confirmed through the years as a genuine person in her own right and she affirms herself in this manner.

The adult- or peer-oriented girl remains where it's safe, embedded in a relation whose structure is determined wholly by others. Any seemingly independent move on her part is sponsored by adults or by esteemed peers. The relation to family or to peers is sufficiently congenial so that she feels no real impetus to move away from these groups. The adult- or peer-oriented girl has little autonomy to bring to her relations.

If early experience with family and peers was not congenial, even this refuge is not available to the adolescent girl. The parents may have been pressuring or neglectful or abandoning. A girl's behavior may have been confirmed very early by her parents as "peculiar" or "bad" or "irrelevant" and she subsequently affirms herself in this manner as anarchic bohemian or delinquent or sick, thereby isolating herself from esteemed peers and being ostracized by them. Repeated "logical" confirmations by family, by peers, and by other adult authorities follow the initial confirmation, then repeated affirmations by the girl, until finally this is what she is, this is her character.

The adolescent types that have been described are empirical types but a girl may have the characteristics of more than one type. The girl, for example, who has been confirmed as both queer and bad is likely to affirm herself as both anarchic bohemian and delinquent.

The power of the confirmation-affirmation process in childhood leads to virtual irreversibility of character formation. The wheels are set in motion very early. This places a heavy burden on parents, who are the products of their own social circumstance. The cycle could be broken by some strong intervention, possibly by establishing radically new relationships away from home or by psychotherapy. Most high school girls have not experienced such intervention.

Finally, looking at the autonomous girl in the light of societal goals, the question arises: should our society foster the confirmation and affirmation of autonomous girls? Is the girl to be regarded as a queer duck if she doesn't conform to her parents and peers? Is she to be told she will be happier as a wife and mother if she learns the prescribed ways of acting and reacting as an appendage to her husband? The answer is as big as life itself. It involves the conservative principle: stability, familiarity, and predictability; and the vital principle: risk, adventure, choice, and passion. The former has to do with reciprocal role relations, the latter, with personal relations. Personal life at its fullest for both male and female rests on the conservative base of reciprocal relation but its vitality rests on the transcendence of this base. Only confirmation and affirmation as autonomous persons permit both the conservative and the vital principle to operate.

appendix

THE EXPERIENCE
OF PARTICIPANT OBSERVATION
AND INTERVIEWING

PARTICIPANT OBSERVATION
WITH THE HOSPITAL GIRLS

At the private hospital

The girl at the private hospital lives with fifteen other girls in a brick pavilion that is detached from the rest of the hospital, with its two hundred patients in all. Most of her activity is confined to the pavilion, except for school in another building, play on the grounds, and scheduled activity with adult patients several evenings a week. She spends half her school day in classes, the other half in occupational therapy. Four days a week she sees a resident psychiatrist for individual psychotherapy. A voluntary recreation program is scheduled after school and she may go off-grounds during the weekend. The psychiatric staff for the sixteen-girl pavilion includes a supervisor, an administrator, and three resident psychiatrists. The pavilion has its own teachers, occupational therapists, case and group workers, nurses, and five attendants on each of three shifts.

My entrance into the pavilion is paved by the psychiatrist-administrator, who tells the girls that a sociologist is coming to do research; that she will keep their confidences; that she is not a staff member and will not have keys.

During the first few weeks I feel somewhat self-conscious, more so with the staff than the girls. There are probably many reasons for this: my own apprehension, a lack of definition of the role I am assuming, a less than enthusiastic acceptance by the staff, and an identification with the girls. I gradually get used to the pavilion, and its members to me. I can enter any room where girls are gathered and for the most part they seem to continue their conversation as though I were not there. (When two girls are alone and I think a third person might be an intruder, I do not enter a room. However, I join threesomes without hesitation.)

In the early period, a girl's trust is transitory—one day I might have it but the next day it might be gone. Except with a few girls, there is no steadily developing relationship but something that has continually to be reachieved. Gradually though, I gain a girl's confidence on a less sporadic basis.

When I enter the recreation room the first day, the girls overwhelm me with questions: "How old are you?" "Do you have your Ph.D.?" "Are you married?" "Do you dance?" They continue to probe during my fifteen-week stay. They seem interested in my marital status and age, want to know why I am not married, and make frequent attempts to "fix me up." Next, they are interested in what I wear, follow daily my change of attire, and express approval or disapproval.

From my dress, their comments wander to other aspects of my physical appearance: my hair, bust measurement, and posture.

They ask questions about my job. What kind of education did I need? How long a period of preparation? Is the salary equivalent to that for a teacher? Who pays me? Was my path in becoming a sociologist a straight one or was it circuitous? If I have a Ph.D., why don't I call myself "Doctor"? Does a Ph.D. give as much satisfaction as a man?

The girls see me essentially as a professional person who is participating in many of their activities and observing what they do. They insist soon after my arrival that I be a participant. They will not accept me on any other terms. I cannot just sit around and observe.

Bonnie asks me if I am going to be at the party the girls are giving for the boys that night. When I say that I am, she responds, "Don't observe.

this: (1) they are often impulsive; (2) they may be flaunting their rebellious behavior for me to see; and (3) I don't appear to do much about what I see or hear. But they are aware that I am present and indicate this by a word or a glance.

"I would like to know you on the outside to find out what you are really like," one of the private hospital girls say to me. The girls at the private hospital see me as a friend. To the girls at the state hospital I am either an adult to be manipulated or a protective maternal figure.

If I have no practical function, perhaps I am there to serve them and can do whatever they wish: will I get them cigarettes, candy, a cup of tea, stamps? If I am unwilling, is it because I don't have the money? Will I call their mothers or grandmothers or aunts? Will I unlock their doors, turn on their lights? Will I go over and tell some of the girls to turn the television up louder? Can they try on my shoes, my bracelet, my watch? Can they wear them to the party tonight? When I don't want my bracelet any more, will I give it to them? May they have my angora vest?

Whether they are manipulating me and seeking out my soft spots, or whether they are testing my acceptance of them I am not always sure. I have the feeling that these are girls whose deprivation has been so great they are trying to fill a bottomless pit. If I do something for them, or get something, they will test for more and more and more. They know that they sometimes make requests that I can't satisfy without disobeying ward regulations, and they know too that I feel uncomfortable and even guilty not acceding to many of their requests when I know that their present existence is so barren.

Some of the girls show a kind of nonverbal relatedness to me. The younger girls, especially, seem to see me as a friendly and possibly a protective mother figure. They hold my hand, walk around with me, sit close to me while watching television, lay their heads in my lap, offer me cookies, dance with me, comb my hair. But the same girls can be very hostile a short time later. A few girls are very demanding of my time and show hurt feelings or scorn when I move on to other girls. These seem to be the girls who prefer adult to peer companionship.

The girls here seem interested in what I do when I am away from the hospital and ask more personal questions than the middle-class girls at the private hospital. Am I going to see my boy friend? Am I going to the movies? What is my boy friend's name? Is that the way I dance with my boy friend? Where do I live? Do I live with my mother? Why don't I? Did my parents give me money to come to New York? If I live alone, do I have anybody to talk to at home? Do I have sexual intercourse with my boy friend?

The girls have some difficulty understanding just what I am doing. I seem to have no practical function. "Is it for fun?" asks Sally. "You're a volunteer," says Eleanor. "Just nosey," says Elizabeth. "A spy," adds Claire.

Elizabeth asks whether I don't find my job boring, just sitting around all day doing nothing. Why don't I go to a hospital where I can really help, where the patients are really sick?

Kitty introduces me to a new attendant, says that I am a sociologist, that I don't work here. A sociologist, she explains, lives with the group so she can find what the hospital management and the girls are like and what they think and talk about.

Lenore asks if you have to go to college to be a sociologist. She thinks she would like to be one. It seems easy.

"Do you like it better here or at the other (private) hospital?" Joyce wants to know. "Which is more violent? Here, isn't it?" She knows that I never saw such fights in my life. She remembers the look on my face several weeks ago when Marian and Claire were fighting.

Overt hostility is sometimes expressed toward me.

"I could beat you up if I wanted to," Joyce says to me when I enter one morning. I agree that she could.

Shelly makes fun of my smile, of how quiet I am. She says that Elizabeth is becoming "collegian" and "conservative" like me. "Conservatives," she explains, are "goodies" who don't do the things that the others do and think they are better than the others.

Marian twists my arm and tries to take my key. I say nothing but hold the key firmly. She gives up. Mabel asks if I am angry with the girls now.

Karen pulls at my bracelet and key string. I become increasingly annoyed and raise my voice: "Stop it, Karen," I insist. "Look at her face!" exclaims Elizabeth incredulously. "I must tell the girls." Elizabeth's statement was not made unpleasantly but rather in the tone of, "Oh, she's human." My expression of anger seems to indicate (1) that I am human; and (2) that if I act "naturally," maybe I am seeing the girls not as "sick" but as ordinary people.

Later, the atmosphere seems to improve. I now intervene more than I have before and I bring in games (for instance, checkers, bingo) each day. I think I show the girls that I do serve a useful function and am interested in how they spend their time. In addition, they seem to respond positively to somebody who is able to "take" so much from them without being angry or vengeful. The idea of a researcher accepting their hostility without responding in similar vein seems somewhat strange to them. The private hospital girls saw this as "being professional" but the state hospital girls have no similar conception.

Elizabeth and Sara tell me that I am very nice. "Sometimes," I admit. "No, all the time," says Sara. "You're always smiling." "You keep being nice," says Elizabeth, "and you have to take so much from the girls. I don't know why you do it." Several girls express surprise that I eat dinner with them after their expressions of hostility the day before; they seem grateful that I do.

But I am greeted by another hostile barrage on the day that a psychologist asks Claire whether "Dr. Cohen" is on her ward. Claire greets me accusingly when I arrive on the ward, "You're a doctor. The psychiatrist told me so. You never told us. You're a spy. You tell the doctors things."

The rumor spreads rapidly that I am a "doctor." I explain that I am a different kind of doctor, a sociologist, not a medical doctor, not a psychiatrist. This seems to them a fine and petty distinction. I suggest that they ask the staff whether I report any of my observations. "They won't tell us," is the immediate response. I give up, and when Claire says, "Hello, Dr. Cohen," I reply, "Hello, Dr. Trott." Claire confesses that she would like to be a doctor when she grows up, a pediatrician.

After that day the girls who continue to bring the "doctor" issue up are those whose confidences I have least been able to obtain.

Claire says to me, "You're a spy. You're a doctor. I don't like you. Yes, I like you. But I don't like doctors and you're a doctor."

During much of the three-month period of participant observation, I come on the ward about 10:30 in the morning and leave about 6:30 in the evening. This eight-hour period is spent with the group except for the brief time I leave to write notes. I never take notes in their presence. I find this absorption in the group too stultifying and isolating, and so I start to eat lunch in the staff dining room in another building. I continue to eat dinner with the girls and to sit with them during their lunch. I spend occasional evenings with the group but do not sleep over, as I had done at the private hospital (and later do at the other state hospital).

My perception of the girls is probably implicit in my discussion of their perception of me. My initiation into the group is more difficult than at the private hospital. At the latter were middle-class girls who could have been my younger sisters or daughters or nieces. I perceive them as such and they perceive me correspondingly. I don't feel the patient-nonpatient gap between us.

The class gap at the state hospital is difficult to transcend. Here are girls living ostensibly in the same world with me but whose past experiences, present values, and future expectations are so different from mine. With them I never pretend to be what I am not. I begin to see them as individuals, and they gradually accept me, middle class and adult (and therefore authority figure) though I am. However, I don't think the gap between us is ever completely closed, that I ever establish rapport or acquire trust in the same measure that I have with the girls at the private hospital.

AT THE OTHER STATE HOSPITAL: MORRISVILLE I arrive on the ward at the second state hospital a few days after a male patient escapes from the hospital and kills a woman in the nearby village. The repercussions are widespread. The director of the hospital cancels his reservations for a trip to Europe, the town conducts several town meetings, and the state investigates. Staff members fear that there will be a toughening of regulations.

It is not surprising, then, that some of the staff suspect that I am a representative from the state government who has come to "spy" on them. The reaction among the staff varies. Some seem cordial and receptive. Some treat me as a "guest." Some are made

so anxious that they stay off the ward. It is informative to compare
my record of the first night I sleep over with the ward daily log.
(I arrive on the ward Monday, sleep over Thursday evening.)

Record of Participant Observer
Thursday, August 21. Evening

Early in the evening I remove my dress from my suitcase, hang it over
a chair (there are no closets in the rooms). While I am in the shower,
Lauren initiates me by putting my dress back into the suitcase. I note its
absence and recognize Lauren's humor. "Where is it, Lauren?" I ask as she
stands in the doorway. Other girls soon join her. After a brief search, I
discover where she put it.

The evening is rather uneventful. For the first hour or two, girls play
jacks, draw, read *True Story,* sew, talk together. Then an old Red Skelton
movie is presented amid much technical difficulty—a bad sound track. I
leave soon after the movie goes on—I find it difficult to watch—go into
one of the offices off the ward to type and read, and return just before the
movie is over. By this time some of the girls are wandering about, others
have gone to sleep in their chairs. "Where were you?" the girls want to
know. They tell me that if I want to read where it is quiet I can read in
my room, I needn't go off the ward. They are telling me, I think, that it
is a pleasant and comforting feeling having an adult on the ward dressed
for bed.

Staff Perception as Reported in The Ward Log.
Thursday Evening. August 21.

Frances really took advantage of the fact we had company on the ward.
Very fresh to Mrs._____ and myself and also [to] Dr._____ and Mrs.
_____. Frances complained she was sick and when doctor came to see her
refused to let her [the doctor] see her. Molly uncooperative during movie.
Said she had a headache but as soon as movie was over said her head was
all right. A few of the girls on the ward tried to show their best behavior
but the majority was very nasty and noisy.

Grace said she fell down on her way to the ice cream machine. She is
not sure what time it was but feels it was between 2:30 and 3:30 P.M. Seen
by Dr._____.

Note. When Miss Cohen undressed for bed, some of the girls went into her room, hid her dress, and she could not find it. Later it turned up in her suitcase. No one knew anything about it.

Ward very noisy all evening.

The next day the ward is very tense. Three girls have been in bed much of the day and now wander in and out of the dayroom describing their ills. Somebody announces that Molly is smothering one of the cats, whereupon she is pounced upon and begins to whine. The attendant informs me that the girls are "acting up" because I, a visitor, am on the ward. The charge nurse, who returns to the ward several times after she has presumably gone for the day, repeats this accusation. When I express surprise, she quickly enumerates other possible causes of tension.

The following Monday morning—I have been on the ward a week—the charge nurse asks the girls about me before my arrival and gives me an account.

"Who is Miss Cohen," she asks them. "A lady," they reply, and then, "a sociologist." "Why is she here," the charge nurse queries. "To observe us," is their response. The charge nurse tells them to ignore Miss Cohen and act as they generally would. Miss Cohen isn't the only one who observes the group. The charge nurse herself observes the group.

Why this acute self-consciousness on the part of staff that I had experienced nowhere else? It takes me several months to realize that the charge nurse sees me as a threat. To her, I am the "visitor," and I have the feeling that if I remained a year or two, I should still be the "visitor" (1) whose knowledge of the ward and the girls is limited; (2) who can be held at least partly responsible for any unfavorable group performance; (3) who probably won't stay long, isn't a permanent fixture, won't ever get settled; and (4) who is unlikely to gain the affection of girls or staff.

The charge nurse informs me that she and the resident on the ward have told a consulting psychiatrist that the therapy group "freezes" when I attend the sessions. I express disagreement. The involvement and articulateness of the girls varies considerably from session to session in the meetings I attend. The charge nurse mumbles something about an overall impression. The resident psychiatrist, when I speak with him, says he had agreed with the charge nurse. I repeat my reaction. He reflects and then says, "It's not the girls, it's us, the staff. It's our problem. We're insecure and we're projecting our own insecurities on to you. And I guess I heard the charge nurse say it so much that I believed it."

"If you knew the girls as I know them," the charge nurse says to me after attending a ward dance, "you would realize how fascinating it was seeing them last night." I have been on the ward for two and a half months. During this period, not only have I been observing the girls but I have been soaking in everything that the nurse can tell me. At the beginning I relate some of my observations to her. This seems to me a legitimate *quid pro quo* that will not interfere with the study. But she doesn't regard this as confidential and repeats some of my findings to the girls, who say to me, "You told the nurse." After this, I rigorously limit my disclosures.

The charge nurse asks one of the supervising psychiatrists if my being there has affected his attitude toward her and her work.

I had the feeling that, had I been a subordinate of the charge nurse, my position would have become untenable and I would have had to leave.[2] I am reminded of the junior nurse, in Stanton and Schwartz' study *The Mental Hospital,* whom the senior nurse sees as threatening because she is becoming too popular with the patients and with staff. The junior nurse resigned.[3]

The senior staff has less of a personal stake in my presence. After a long interview with the nursing supervisor, I alleviate the anxiety that she has expressed to some staff members and she is friendly and cooperative. With one supervising psychiatrist who spends a great deal of time on the ward I have the added experience of observing the group through his very alert and well-trained eyes.

The girls here ask me much the same questions as were asked at Endicott. They appear to test me, to try to discover where my allegiance lies. When we are in the yard the first afternoon, they ask me to keep talking to the attendant so she won't notice they are swinging so high and that they sit two-on-a-swing facing each other.

There seem fewer spontaneous overtures toward me among the

[2] This is the same nurse described on p. 82 of Chapter Six, a woman dedicated very constructively and imaginatively to the welfare of her young charges.

[3] Alfred H. Stanton and Morris S. Schwartz, *The Mental Hospital* (New York: Basic Books, Inc., Publishers, 1954).

girls at Morrisville than at the other two hospitals. For some time there is more politeness, hesitancy, and self-consciousness in relation to me. I remain for a long time the "visitor" who doesn't quite fit in. There is more restraint in expressing suspicion. When, at length, I am dubbed a "spy," the accusation is made more frequently here. I feel that this is partially a role that has seeped down from the staff, who more often than in the other institutions see me as a threatening person.

Carmen asks me if it is true that I find out about the girls and tell the court what happens. This is what she has heard from the staff downstairs. Frances tells her not to be an instigator. Lauren says she heard from one of the staff that I am writing a book. When do I take notes? "Do you keep it all in your head?" she wants to know, and then asks, "Aren't all groups pretty much alike?"

It becomes clearer to me here than at the other hospitals that since my position is such an ambiguous one—I am not staff and I am not girl—carrying no authority, I am like a sponge that can be used to soak up the girls' hostility and frustration.

A dance is to be held one evening and the seventeen oldest girls are permitted to attend. Mistakenly I ask Agnes if she is going to the dance. "No, bitch," she retorts as she picks up some books and throws them at me. I show little response though I duck the books, and she puts her arms around me and kisses me. (Agnes presumably can't express her grievances to her mother; she even finds it difficult to thwart her play mother. She feels free enough on the ward and with me so that she can throw books and then, possibly overcome with guilt, she rushes over and kisses me.)

Lois taunts the girls at dinner. She has had no word from her mother who was to take her home for a visit. She turns to me. "Don't smile at me," she growls. "I'm not a man."

I enter a group therapy session and am greeted with, "Oh, her again. Why does she have to spy on us all the time? I don't like her. . . . yes I do. . . . No I don't."

On the other hand, the relationship between us becomes increasingly personal and trusting. The girls ask many times over the same personal questions that I am asked at the other state hospital. They express interest in my social life, my sex life, my appearance, and my clothes. Almost everything that I wear on the ward is discussed, criticized, analyzed, and recommendations made. Some of the girls, in an embarrassed tone, ask me if I will "go with them." I have become something of a model to some of them and this is how they express their acceptance.

The girls are excited at my sleeping on the ward. This is something new. Long after I stop my daily visits, girls still ask when I will sleep over. "Why do you want me to sleep over, Rachel?" I ask, and anticipate the answer, "It reminds me of home and my mother."

I think I experience more anxiety here than in the two other groups of adolescent girls. What is different about this group?

"Did they ever accept you?" one of the supervising psychiatrists asks me at the termination of my stay. Nobody had asked that question at the other hospitals. Acceptance-nonacceptance: this is an important issue on the ward. Several attendants speak about their attempts to curry favor with the girls. Whom do the girls like, whom don't they like? The tone is set by the charge nurse; it is very important for her to be "queen bee." I feel freer and more relaxed in the evening when she is off the ward.

I find that, despite the occasional outbursts and expressions of aggression that the girls direct against me, and despite my anxiety over staff reactions, I can approach the girls more easily, as time goes on, than at Endicott. They are less the "toughies," for some reason less scarred by human contact, so that we can eventually establish a closer rapport. It may be the ward itself, its pleasantness and charm, that makes this rapport possible, as well as the interest that the charge nurse and psychiatrist exhibit in the girls.

INTERVIEWING IN THE COMMUNITY

The suburban girls

When I call the girls to arrange for interviews, I explain that I am a sociologist who has concluded a study of girls in three mental hospitals and I now want to interview girls in the community to get a picture of what high school girls in general are like. An occasional girl asks about the sponsorship of the study and the possibility of publication. Almost every girl indicates a willingness to be interviewed. About one out of five mothers (only one father) is called to the telephone by her daughter or calls me later to ask what the study is about. Though a few mothers telephone me if the interview extends long beyond the scheduled time, no suburban parent vetoes her daughter's participation in the study.

I pick up most of the suburban girls by car and bring them to my home. The girls whom I arrange to pick up are always ready at the scheduled time. The setting for the interview is informal— my living room or kitchen. A child often accompanies me in the car and is nearby at play as we talk. Five girls prefer to be interviewed in their own homes, usually for reasons of convenience, but at least once because of a mother's uncertainty about permitting the trip to the unknown home.

All girls talk more or less freely and seem to like to be interviewed. "Yes, I know about it," is a typical comment when I call on the phone for the first time. "You interviewed my friend." As the interview proceeds, the girl usually shows a pervasive interest and absorption. I find that the middle-class girl talks well when she is interviewed alone.

Through daily participant observation of hospital girls for almost a year, I have gained some insight into the important aspects of a girl's living, on the basis of which an interview schedule is prepared. I have no hard-and-fast procedure for asking questions. I let the interview proceed at its own pace, one question leading to another, so that no two interviews are conducted in precisely the same manner. The only requirement is that at the conclusion of the interview all areas of study will have been covered. Often the questions on sex are asked last, but some girls, by their answers or comments, lead to these questions earlier in the interview. With the Negro girl, I often wait until well into the interview to ask questions about race but this too is no hard-and-fast rule. The interview takes from one to two and a half hours.

The interview seems to open up new areas of thinking for many girls. A girl frequently remarks that she was never asked such questions before—very rarely has anybody talked to her about personal matters at such length—and she had never thought about many of these matters. "Are my answers very different from other girls'?" a few aspirants for autonomy want to know, and are resentful when I ask a question by indirection about what girls "in general" do or think or feel. The autonomous girl wants to be sure that she is speaking for herself and not mouthing the opinions of the group.

The city girls

I am introduced to some city girls whose names I have been given when they visit the local community centers. I make an appointment by phone with the others. All of the city girls are interviewed at the two community centers. Often greater effort has to be exerted before the interview begins in order to win the confidence of the city girl than was necessary for the suburban girl. I frequently have to call several times and occasionally have to arrange for another appointment.

The lower-class city girls are usually seen two at a time. The girl seems to talk more openly when one of her peers is present, one girl's comments "freeing" the other girl. Initially a girl may simply express agreement with her more vocal friend but once she has begun to talk, she can more easily be drawn out in the presence of her peer than if she were alone with me.

After the interview begins, the rapport with the city girls does not seem to me to be less than with the suburban girls. Even the most impulsive lower-class girl, who smokes during the interview and experiences some interference from boys outside the window, turns her back to the boys and continues to talk. She goes out once during the interview to get another cigarette and I am somewhat doubtful that she will return, but she does come back and is willing to talk as long as I will listen.

In the community sample, after a girl's name is obtained, every effort is made to interview her. The refusal rate is less than 5 per cent of the girls who were reached. No girl directly refuses to be interviewed, but I regard as a refusal any instance where a girl does not keep her appointment and cannot be reached after repeated tries, or when an interview has begun but is not completed. There are two parental refusals—these come from mothers of city girls.

INDEX